GARDEN DECORATION

HOUSE & GARDEN BOOK OF

GARDEN DECORATION

Edited by Peter Coats

A Studio Book

THE VIKING PRESS · NEW YORK

Copyright © 1970 by Condé Nast Publications Ltd, London
All rights reserved

Published in 1970 by The Viking Press, Inc.
625 Madison Avenue, New York, N.Y. 10022

Second Printing, December 1970

SBN 670-37969-7

Library of Congress catalog card number: 76-119782

Printed and bound in Great Britain

CONTENTS

Acknowledgements: Peter Coats took most of the photographs for this book. Other photographers represented are: Jacques Bachmann, Ralph Bailey, Beadle, Franz Benedikter, Jacques Boucher, Emmett Bright, John Brookes, Dainesi, Anthony Denney, Max Eckert, Richard Einzig, Espen-Hansen, Fink, Roger Gain, Paul Genereux, William Grigsby, Miles Hadfield, Brodrick Haldane, Harrison, Ryle Hodges, Horst, H. R. Jowett, Thomas Kernan, Marc Lacroix, Jean-Claude Lamontagne, Tom Leonard, Fred Lyon, Daniel Maresco Pearce, Maris, Patrick Matthews, Joseph Molitor, James Mortimer, Ugo Mulas, Naar, Primois-Pinto, Howard Robinson, Michael Scott Brown, Simmonds, Edwin Smith, Taloumis, Barry Weller, Colin Westwood, Julian White, Michael Wickham, Ray Williams, John Wingrove and Tom Yee. The illustration on page 10 is reproduced by kind permission of the Trustees of the British Museum.

INTRODUCTION

This is not the book for those in search of knowledge as to how to kill slugs, or how far apart to space their carrot seedlings. It is not a book for gardeners who have a black-spot problem or whose yew hedge has honey-fungus; they should look elsewhere for the cures. Plantsmen whose Magnolia campbellii has failed to flower must choose a more practical work. The ghost of William Robinson, who deplored the ornamentation of the gardens at Versailles, definitely would not approve.

For though this book is about gardens, it is not, primarily, about plants. It is a book about garden decoration. Some of the pictures it contains are of very grand, royal gardens. It could be said, therefore that it is more about Kings than cabbages. Versailles, the greatest garden in the world, was the creation of a King. The garden at Würzburg was a Grand-Ducal garden. And though it may be asked 'what on earth' (for all gardens, however Grand-Ducal, are earth-bound) 'what on earth can we learn from these rich men's pleasure grounds, these Kings' parterres?' the answer is, in one word, 'much'. You can learn that a lawn, however small, should have a shape, like Louis XIV's *tapis vert*, and not be just an amorphous space between two flower-beds. You can be inspired by the well-placed statues at Würzburg or the trellis-work arbours in the marvellous garden at Schwetzingen, to have something of the sort, however small, in your own garden. And the water-toys of Tivoli, Frascati or the Villa Lante (the names alone speak the language of fountains) can recommend to you the value of water, and the blessing on rare hot days, of a falling spray.

The concept of man-made additions coming to the aid of nature is

1 'A lawn, however small, should have a shape, like Louis XIV's *tapis vert* . . .' The famous stretch of turf at Versailles lies beyond the circular pool of Latona
2 A sculpture of children in a leafy setting in the baroque garden of the Residenz at Würzburg

1

2

The twin pavilions of the Villa Lante near Viterbo in Italy overlook a garden which has been famous since the seventeenth century. The central fountain with its quartette of giants was designed by Giovanni di Bologna. Montaigne thought the Villa Lante gardens finer than those at Tivoli

not a new one. It is as old as time itself. If, in the garden of Eden, there was no Interior decoration for the Exterior to echo, it is because there was no Interior. The whole of Adam's world was a garden. He had no panelling, no architraves, no pediments, to suggest temples of trellis work, no parquet to suggest parterres, no indoor seats to inspire outdoor ones.

For that is the subject of this book—how man has been inspired to reproduce the features which he has used in his home not only to embellish, but also to render more comfortable, the immediate area outdoors.

The process, if it did not start with Adam, began long ago. One of the seven wonders of the world were the Hanging Gardens of Babylon,

those gardens and terraces of limestone and breccia slabs, where King Nabopolasser and his court could take the Assyrian air.

Gardens, with tanks of lotos, adjoined the palaces of Karnak, and there is a carving of a gardener of Ancient Egypt, at work in his garden, in the Valley of the Kings. Four hundred years before Christ, on a loggia in Athens, City of Violets, Plato held his immortal discussions with Socrates. And in Roman days Pliny described the garden which was an extension to his villa in Herculaneum. Much of Pliny's *Natural History* deals with the subject of Botany: and his garden sounds very much in the spirit of this book—carpeted with box-bordered parterres, walled in evergreens, and curtained with the golden foliage of vines.

No garden survived the Dark Ages, and it was not until the thirteenth

1

1 The Garden of Mirth, in an illustration to Chaucer's fourteenth century 'Romaunt de la Rose'
2 A gothic doorway to a courtyard
3 A sunken garden at Hampton Court in a seventeenth century design
4 At the Villa Marlia near Lucca there is this garden house with tessellated paving and a graceful marble vase
5 An elaborate scroll-work parterre of raked gravel and turf, in typical eighteenth-century style, at Versailles. Such sophisticated garden designs owe something to the Tudor knot

century that times were peaceful enough for the creation and maintenance of gardens that were dedicated to pleasure and recreation only, and not to growing food. In the British Museum there is an illustration to Chaucer's *Romaunt de la Rose* of a garden in the Middle Ages which contains many of the elements we look for in the well-furnished, well-decorated garden of today. It is shown on this page. The lover in search of his heroine seeks entry to the Garden of Mirth. A maiden leads him to as neat and practical a gate as anyone could devise today. Inside, within quite a small area, the garden contains several well-planned, well-placed features—elegant trellis fencing, a carpet-like pattern of flower beds, well spaced trees (then, as now, important furniture for any garden). Neat paving stones held firm by iron clamps surround a pool

4, 5

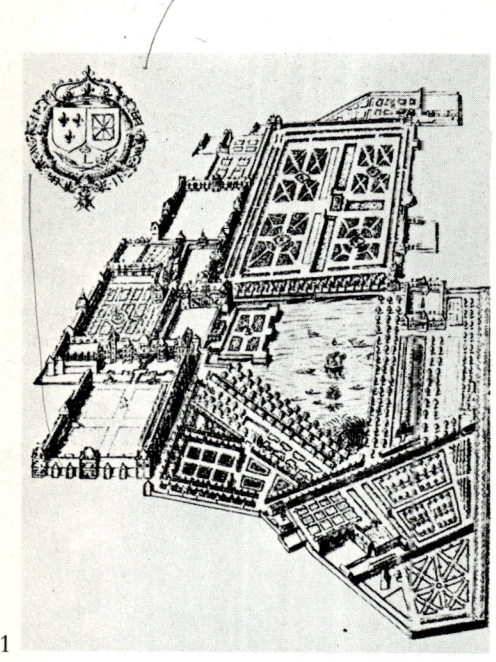

1

1 Jacques Androuet de Cerceau lived from 1515 until 1584. He left many designs for garden lay-out; this one is of the garden at Fontainebleau
2 In the garden at Hautefort in the Dordogne (where the château was recently destroyed by fire) there is this parterre inspired by one at Castello Gandolfo, the Pope's country palace. The intricate pattern of this splendid green carpet is carried out in box and lonicera, and the whole is enclosed in a doored and windowed hedge of yew. A well-furnished garden indeed

fed by eight falling jets of water. Beyond is a castellated wall, but on the inward side there is a fence clothed with a tapestry of roses. This garden in the *Romaunt de la Rose*, contains a group of happy people, reading, singing and playing the lute. It is a Garden of Mirth indeed, but a garden of fantasy, of imagination too. It is doubtful whether any such garden ever existed, but already five centuries ago it represented an ideal.

Shakespeare, writing two hundred years later, was intensely garden-minded, and there are many references to gardens in his plays. For Hamlet, in his discontent, the world was an unweeded garden, and though a garden was a refuge and place of recreation for the neglected Queen Isabel, her sorrows made her forget her manners to such an extent as rudely to refer to the gardener as 'Thou lesser thing than earth,' an incivility generously rewarded with 'a bank of rue, even for ruth, . . . in the remembrance of a weeping queen'.

But it was a great contemporary of Shakespeare who pointed the way to garden decoration in one of his greatest, and certainly the best known of all his essays—Francis Bacon. His essay *Of Gardens* is so full of light-hearted ideas on garden decor that at one point Bacon excuses his suggestions (for 'figures, with divers coloured earth') with the words 'you may see as good sights many times in tarts'. But other of his notions for the embellishment of gardens are as practical today as they were in the sixteenth century. 'Paths planted with burnet, with thyme and water mints; therefore you are to set whole alleys of them, to have the pleasure, when you walk or tread . . .'. He 'liked well, little low hedges, round like welts, with some pretty pyramids'. In Bacon's opinion 'fountains are a great beauty and refreshment: but pools mar all, and make the garden unwholesome and full of flies and frogs'. His advice, to supply the garden with gravelled walks for dryness, arbours for shade, and pots of pinks and gilly flowers 'outside and under the windows', still rings sensible and true.

There are so many references to garden decoration in Bacon's essay that one must ration oneself in quoting them.

A garden device which has survived in many forms and versions—the knot—was an innovation in Chaucer's time.

A knot garden, in Elizabethan gardens, was an elaborate carpet garden, or parterre, of interwoven (knotted) low hedges of box, lavender or ivy, containing beds of flowers. There is an elaborately reconstructed knot garden at Hampton Court, and it is a style of gardening which was the predecessor of carpet bedding at its best, or worst, down to our own time. The great scrolled designs of Versailles and Vaux-le-Vicomte owe something to the Tudor knot, as do the Victorian mosaic gardens which Disraeli derided. At its best, a well-designed knot, like the one at Hampton Court, can make a most effective outdoor carpet—at its worst, when perpetrated in red salvias, brassy calceolarias and regimented echeverias, it can be a loathsome thing, God wot.

2

3

1 A simple outbuilding (which is, in fact, a garage) is embellished by a painted niche and classical statue. At Maenan Hall, Llanrwst, North Wales
2 A boat suggests adventure and offers the most relaxing of occupations—a row under overhanging trees
3 For the Arabs water was the 'music of the Alhambra'. The patio de la Riadh, with its arching fountains

Long before the first knot garden was laid out in England, there had been a Renaissance in Italy in garden design as in everything else. Charles VIII of France, in 1495, wrote enthusiastically from Naples to his family in Paris: 'You can not imagine what beautiful gardens I have seen . . . for on my word, it seems as though only Adam and Eve were wanting to make an earthly paradise, so full are they of rare and beautiful things.' The delighted French king soon afterwards imported craftsmen from Italy to make gardens for the royal Châteaux of France like those he had admired in Italy. In Touraine and around Paris, fountains flowed in imitation of the waters of Frascati, bosquets of clipped trees, sky-ceiled salons, were planted to rival those at Villa Lante and statues and balustrading devised to match the gardens laid out in 1549 by the Cardinal of Ferrara at Tivoli.

Designs for these early French gardens, which display garden embellishment at its very best, survive in the crystal engravings of Jacques Androuet du Cerceau (1515–1584). Few gardens of that date survive in France, but at the Château of Hautefort, page 13, there is an inspired reconstruction, which with its subtle relationship between the visual

reward of architecture, and the practical need for growing space, allows us to appreciate to the full the good sense and logic of the French—qualities which controlled, and held in check, their enthusiasm for the early intoxication with the ideas wafted from lighter-hearted, and, incidentally, warmer, Italy.

If Italian gardens gave the lead in the fifteenth and sixteenth century, by the seventeenth they were eclipsed completely by the new, great gardens of France. Here the art of garden decoration surely reached its peak. The gardens of Versailles and of Vaux le Vicomte, are the two perfectly furnished gardens of the world, and they display every concept of garden embellishment at its best. The celebrated *tapis-vert*, a carpet of turf, has already been noted. But these two heroic gardens are carpeted 'throughout' in perfectly proportioned lawns and terraces, they are curtained with walls of verdure and furnished with perfectly tailored trees and statues, Versailles particularly, for the jealous Louis XIV robbed Fouquet's garden of many of its ornaments. Gardens within gardens, such as the grove surrounding the Bassin du Dragon at Versailles, offer retreats for meditation, repose or dalliance. *Pièces d'eau* reflect the sky, as they could do in the smallest garden, and fountains provide rising and falling veils and sprays of water. Water is of inestimable value in beautifying gardens.

For the Arabs, water was the 'music of the Alhambra', where there are a series of courtyard gardens which are models of garden decor. The Patio of the Myrtles (*de los Arrayanes*) and the Court of the Lions in Granada may seem a far cry from our own gardens of today, but their fountains, miniature canals and pools speak softly but insistently for themselves, and invite emulation.

The Romantic Revival in the early eighteenth century was born of the genius of the banker, Henry Hoare, who created one of England's greatest gardens, Stourhead. It was a movement which, with one hand, gave much to garden decor, but with the other took much away. The Return to Nature swept away the neat parterres of box and flower beds, the pergolaed walks. Statuary and terraces became, overnight, unfashionable. Topiary, so long furniture of the well-ordered garden, suddenly seemed out of date. Addision deplored 'the mark of scissors on every plant and bush' and in a well-known passage (in the *Guardian*, 1713) Alexander Pope described an imaginary sale at which the items included '. . . a quick set hedge shot up into a porcupine, and an old maid of honour in wormwood . . .'

The work of sharp pens was followed quickly by the execution of sharp axes, and gardens everywhere, in their full maturity and beauty, disappeared—among them a splendid box parterre at Hampton Court; but that was not for reasons of taste, but rather reasons of State. The smell of box made Queen Anne sneeze.

But the Romantic Revival, the Return to Nature, though it destroyed

1 Dovecotes have been decorative features of gardens for centuries; long since the days when they filled the practical purpose of housing pigeons used for food. This one of white wood, thatched with reed is in a garden in Scarsdale, N.Y.
2 For contrast, a sculptural dovecote in the modern idiom, by Ewen Macleod, in a Sussex garden

A garden seat which might have been designed by William Kent, flanked by statues, in a setting of meticulously tailored topiary at Bodnant in North Wales

much, conferred some benefits on gardeners whose eyes were discomforted by nature completely unadorned. The garden at Stourhead, first man-made landscape, is starred with temples, grottos, and cottages ornés aplenty.

The landscape-garden, or English park, for they are of the same conception, is Britain's one contribution to the art forms of the world. There is no place in the introduction to a book illustrating garden decor such as this, to enlarge on how the English park evolved, or to do more than salute in passing the three high priests of the romantic cult. First, William Kent (1685–1748) of whom Horace Walpole said 'he leaped the fence, and saw that all Nature was a garden'. The garden at Rousham in Oxfordshire, with its winding walks, statues, and eye-catchers, is one of the few Kent creations to survive. Second of the three names in eighteenth-century garden design to acclaim is that of Lancelot Brown (1716–1783) whose hand weighed heavily on the surviving gardens of the preceding age, but who created some of the most exquisite parks in

England. His well-known pseudonym, Capability, derived from his customary remark on being invited to make his suggestions, 'Let us examine the capabilities of the site.' More than any other garden designer, Capability Brown used the then new device of the ha-ha, or sunk fence, to co-opt the surrounding countryside, and make it a blending framework for his parks. Last great name in our trio is Humphry Repton (1752–1818) who carried on the work of Kent and Brown and completed the change from the ordered, artificial, formal gardens of the late seventeenth and early eighteenth century, to the natural parks and gardens of the Romantic Revival.

In any book on garden decoration these three names deserve a place. For as pictures are to a room, or tapestry or mural paintings to a room's walls, so the surrounding landscape must be to a garden. And in any description of man's additions to the garden, mention should surely be made of the names of the creators of the English Park, englischer Garten or parco inglese.

19

1

But though the Romantic Revival was a Return to Nature, it was the least natural thing in the world. And there is as much artifice in the thought which conceived, say, 'the opening and retiring shades of Venus' Vale' at Rousham, or the plantations at Blenheim, as there ever was in the conception of the topiary garden at Levens, which mercifully still exists, or the neat box-bordered parterres at Hampton Court planted with tulips and ornamented with vases of blue-and-white Delft which were the delight of William and Mary, and which have long since disappeared. There is a picture of Levens above.

In the early days of the nineteenth century there appeared a book which must be the delight of all lovers of garden ornament: *Phantasien* or the *Petit Magasin ou Receuil d'idées d'une execution peu dispensieuse*, by J. G. Grohmann, publisher and professor of philosophy at Leipzig. Our chapter on Summer Houses contains many of the illustrations. At its publication garden ornament, after half a century of censure, seemed once more to be about to catch the fancy of the cognoscente. Herr

2

3

Grohmann's book can have few rivals for fantaisie and imagination. But one wonders if many of the enchanting ideas he offers ever achieved reality—how many of his dreams came true? And yet the addition of his simplest suggestions would lend enchantment to the view. Many of them are as suitable additions to the smaller, more labour-starved gardens of today, as to any of the more spacious gardens of the past.

In Victorian times, taste changed. It did not disappear, for the Victorians had a lot of taste, almost all of it bad. Expressionless, sentimental statues in doughy composition; prudently draped maidens, sexless children and mournful dogs took their place in gardens. Acres of greensward were cut up into geometric rose-beds, and paths were gravelled with white granite chippings such as are found on graves. Carpet bedding at its most garish was the rage.

It is not until within living memory that things improved. The great William Robinson censured the garden at Versailles as having '. . . squirting water in an immoderate degree, trees in tubs as an accom-

1 Some of the most spectacular topiary in the world is to be found in the garden of Levens Hall in Westmoreland. The garden was laid out by a Frenchman, Guillaume Beaumont, gardener to James II
2 A round garden seat shaded by an umbrella from an early nineteenth century book on garden ornament
3 One of the only gardens laid out by William Kent (1655–1748) to survive much as he left it, is at Rousham in Oxfordshire. This arcade is in grey stone and is known as Praeneste from a similarity to the Temple of Fortune at Palestrina (Praeneste in ancient times). The urn and its plinth are in odd, but pleasing, proportion

1 'Few of Miss Jekyll's . . . gardens . . . were without their presiding statues, their *genii loci*. . .

2 Several elements of good garden decoration are displayed in this picture of the Dutch royal castle of Warmelo. The curtains of roses are mirrored in the moat, of which the water is enhanced, but not smothered, by lilies; and a topiary yew acts as keystone to the whole

paniment, and perhaps griffins and endless plasterwork and stonework . . .'

But Robinson was such a good gardener in other ways (after all he was the inventor of the herbaceous border) that one can be indulgent: *Tous les goûts sont dans la nature*. His more broadminded friend and colleague Gertrude Jekyll welcomed architecture in gardens, and was quite alive to the pictorial value of the well-placed statue. No one appreciated more the romantic look of moss-carpeted steps, or vine-curtained gateways. No one, in the design of her gardens, could place a summer house more skilfully than Miss Jekyll, or more appreciate the merits of a lily-pond. Of gardens Miss Jekyll once wrote: 'Given the same space of ground and the same material they may either be fashioned into a dream of beauty, a place of perfect rest and refreshment of mind and body—a series of soul-satisfying pictures, or they may be so misused that everything is jarring and unpleasing.'

Few of Miss Jekyll's courtyard gardens, a form of gardening at which she excelled, were without their presiding statues, their *genii loci*. She loved pergolas and the chance they offered, not only of chequered light and shade, but also for growing interesting, and what one might well call, furnishing plants—wistaria, vines, clematis and such. Paving was one of her abiding interests, and brick alternating with cobbles, or paving stones with tiles, made the groundwork of her gardens. But she was always practical, and in one of her books she offers advice on beautifying a roof of galvanized iron with a layer of peaty earth and a planting of stonecrop.

'A combination of common sense and sincerity of purpose, sense of beauty and artistic knowledge . . . can make plain ground and growing things into a year long succession of living pictures . . .' These words of Gertrude Jekyll's, written half a century ago, are as true today as ever. Though, as Bacon tells us, it was not men who first planted a garden, it is man's additions to nature that make the success of a garden today. A clematis depends for its effect on a graceful support, the flowering rose is enhanced by a setting of turf or the background of a grey stone wall. A reddening vine is nowhere so telling as when it canopies a chiselled Ganymede. And in a larger context, a landscape gains immeasurably from being seen beyond a balustrade, as any small garden gains from being seen from the added height of steps. The eye is caught and held by a temple reflected in a lake, or by the sky reflected in a lily pond; the most modest town garden is enlivened by one piece of sculpture.

Though many of us still have gardens, few of us have gardeners. Sculpture, a summerhouse, a fountain, a terrace or a flight of steps, once installed, need little upkeep. To contradict the French dictum *Rien ne dure comme le provisoire*, in garden design today it might be said that nothing lasts—and needs less maintenance—than the permanent.

PETER COATS

TERRACES AND ROOFGARDENS

make an attractive fine-weather extension to the living area of the house

Jonathan Swift, in his *Imitation of Horace* wished for

> A river at my garden's end
> A terrace walk . . . and half a rood
> Of land, set out to plant a wood

But the terrace he dreamed of was not the sort of terrace we think of to-day—it was more probably a high walk, like the ones at Polesdon Lacey or at Muncaster in Cumberland, from whence a view of the surrounding countryside could be obtained, or of the outlying portions of the garden. It was primarily a point of vantage. In Northern countries, at least, terraces, in the form of paved sitting-out places near the house, were a later invention. Elizabethan houses were surrounded by rough lawn or gravel paths and in the eighteenth century landscape gardeners preferred the park to sweep right up to the walls of the house.

It was the Victorians, inventive and always conscious of their creature comforts, who devised the terrace for walking and occasional sitting out. For them, as for us, a terrace offered extra living space in summer and a part of the garden in winter which could be visited dry-shod.

But, for satisfactory outdoor living, even the bold Victorians surely needed a warmer climate than that of Northern Europe? For villas in the South of France, and houses in Italy and Spain, terraces were necessities and in constant use, but in Northern gardens? For sitting out, for meals or drinks *al fresco*, surely our climate was *troppo fresco* altogether, and it would be safer not to attempt terrace-life at all, or to restrict it to tea under the cedar in a heat wave or inside a summer house

1 The addition of a feature like this lion at Weston Park in Staffordshire gives interest to any terrace. Urns or tubs of flowers are often effectively used in this way

2 A terrace, well furnished with rocking chairs and curved stonework seat, comfortably cushioned, overlooks the bay of Formentor. The Villa Ivanovic, in Majorca

1

or gazebo. But in the last half century, though our northern climates have not changed, we seem to have grown more adventurous. For many weeks every summer it is possible, painless, and often pleasant to sit outdoors: and with the development of new, light and well-designed garden furniture, a terrace can make an attractive extension to the living area of the house.

From the aesthetic point of view paving near the house is of great value. Though expensive to lay, once laid it asks for no upkeep and acts as a link between the house and the garden around it in a pleasing and logical way. A terrace extends to outdoors the ordered neatness of indoors.

But where should the architect, or stone-mason yield control to the gardener? It is this question to which natural good taste and an eye for example must supply the answer. A half-timbered cottage can have a terrace of brick or informally laid stone. But so called crazy-paving looks completely out of place outside a formal Georgian or Regency villa.

Terraces can be built of a variety of materials—some expensive, some comparatively cheap. Originality can be exercised in the choice of stone, brick, cobbles or old stable setts. Combinations, such as paving with bricks, cobbles with York stone, can be conjured to make attractive patterns. These different groundworks are particularly useful to give character to small town gardens. Lessons can be learned from the Japanese in the use of sea-washed pebbles, and from experienced gardeners such as the two late, great ladies of gardening, Gertrude Jekyll and Victoria Sackville West, in the use of mat-forming plants between the terrace stones.

Brick as a terracing material has the great advantage of being able to be laid in different patterns—simply, in two's or three's, or in a herring bone pattern as shown in the picture on page 40. But good hard well-burnt bricks should be chosen. For a terrace 16 ft. by 40 ft., at least 2000 bricks would be needed if these were laid flat. If laid on edge, which gives a much better appearance, almost 4000 bricks would be necessary —an extra expense, but with a far better-looking terrace as the result. Ideally, bricks should be laid on concrete—to discourage deep-rooted weeds. But they can also be laid in sand. In either case, if cement is used in pointing them, a groove an inch deep should be left to allow for moss to take root between. Here and there, on parts of the terrace not constantly walked on, spaces can be left, for an informal effect, for low growing plants, such as dianthus, thyme and acaena.

Old York stone makes the ideal terrace and sometimes old paving stones can be acquired, at a price, from a local authority or demolition firm; new York stone is more expensive, but has the advantage of being obtainable cut to size. Whatever stone is used, it should be laid on sand, or concrete, and a mixture of sand and cement brushed into the crevices

1 Hydrangeas in pots of terracotta give a look of luxuriance to this terrace which is neatly paved in brick laid lengthways

2 A monkey-seat from the Veneto where such whimsical garden ornaments (as well as more serious statuary in the eighteenth-century style) are still carved from the soft stone of the Euganean Hills

2

1

1 Furniture of white wire contrasts well with old Cotswold walls and grey paving stones on the terrace at Alderley Grange in Gloucestershire

2 The slightest change of levels makes all the difference in a small town garden. Here three steps lead up from a sunk, well-furnished terrace to the lawn above

3 Recently several firms have started to reproduce Victorian garden furniture such as the chairs in this picture

and watered in, with a fine-rosed watering can.

Artificial paving can be had in the form of concrete slabs. These can be found with many different surfaces; they can be smooth, or given a rough textured surface by being made of different aggregates. A combination of different patterns can be most effective. Also obtainable are paving stones of artificial stone in different colours—varying from olive green to warm pink. But these coloured slabs should be used with the greatest caution. Nothing can spoil the look of a terrace, for which an appearance of dignity and permanence is essential, more than the use of cheap-looking materials.

Roof Gardens

It is important to remember that any roof garden should be arranged so that it looks its best from the windows which open on to it. For the ideal roof garden is the last of a *defilé* of rooms, providing the view at

2

the end. Roof gardens come into their own in winter and early spring, and though they are surely more colourful in summer, it is more in winter and in spring that the roof gardener realizes how specially lucky he is.

The moment when a roof garden is most appreciated is when the leaves have fallen and it is cold outside; comfortably seated in front of your fire you look out of the window, and your delighted eye falls on a pleasing vista of carefully-chosen green leaves. For that is what a well-dressed roof garden ought to provide. If the weather is bad you can remain comfortably indoors; no need to go to the park, no need to get out the car and drive to the country—you have your own country at home, and you can see it without stirring.

Of course, as spring advances the benefits the town dweller receives from his roof garden are more spectacular. There are the first flowers. Species iris such as Iris stylosa and Iris reticulata make their courageous

3

debut, followed by daffodils and the early tulips. Before long the weather will be fine enough for meals outside. . . .

In summer a roof garden, if carefully planted, can be a five-month-long festival of colour. Geraniums, roses, clematis and petunias make a kaleidoscopic pattern in the sunlight, while white tobacco flowers show up romantically at night, and scent the air around.

After the summer holiday (and it is important to remember to arrange to have your roof garden watered while you are away), you may find that some tidying up will be necessary. But if the weather is kind, there will be a last autumnal burst of flowers to brighten your return, before winter sets in, and the permanent decoration of different greens, which have acted loyally all summer as a background to your flowers, comes once more into its own.

For a successful roof garden it is essential to have protection from wind, as well as from unwelcome observers (you might want to sun-bathe). For windbreaks there are reinforced, frosted-glass walls, wattle fencing and close trellis work. But whatever walling you choose for your roof garden it must first of all be wind-, as well as peep-proof. Trellis work gives an opportunity to grow vines, Virginia creeper and above all ivies, the dark green, golden or variegated varieties. Ivies, and indeed all evergreens, are standbys for the well-dressed roof garden. But whatever you plant, provide them with deep, well-drained containers, either in the form of outsize window boxes or of large tubs and flower pots. These should contain a suitable mixture of soil, preferably with a proportion of moisture-retaining peat. Any soil in close containers dries out quickly, and watering is as important for a roof garden as for any other town plot. This is a point which is extremely important, and often neglected.

Should you choose to have built-up borders round the edge of your roof garden, the faces of these can be attractively camouflaged with trellis work, bark or with low hedges set in separate oblong containers. These too need regular watering.

It goes without saying that there are certain technical problems to be faced in constructing a roof garden. First overall weight, and secondly drainage. For the question of weight it would be best to consult the architect of the building, but generally the weight permitted is about 400 lbs to the square yard.

The question of drainage is equally important, not only the drainage of water used in watering the plants, but also the disposal of rain water. And while on the subject of rain water, all plants benefit enormously by being watered with this, rather than with city tap water, which is highly chlorinated. So if you can arrange a tank to preserve rain water so much the better. All flower pots and other containers should contain drainage crocks, and, of course, have holes to allow the water to escape. Built-in containers should be strongly constructed to withstand freezing out.

High above an Italian factory is this roof garden designed by Professor Pietro Porcinai. Exotic plants clothe the walls and fill the flower beds, and orange trees flourish. The drawing is by Rosemary Grimble

1, 2

1 A roof terrace in Neuilly, well-furnished with raised borders of foliage shrubs, white painted, blue cushioned chairs, and a swimming pool to reflect the Paris sky. The garden was planned by M. J. Vidal and L. Vitorge was the architect

2 Immaculately laid marble paving with concrete rafters overhead, and greenery kept within strict bounds, make the chastest décor. The table and chairs are of plastic claritex

Pots containing different soil mixtures enable the more horticultur-ally-minded roof gardener to grow different kinds of plants. Pots of acid soil can be arranged for rhododendrons and camellias, while lime-loving plants such as peonies and miniature lilacs can be given the alkali soil mixture which suits them best.

Box trees are not advisable for roof gardens, though their tailored shapes look elegant, and lend style to any arrangement of plants: but with their roots confined in pots box leaves eventually turn yellow; clipped bays are more satisfactory, and their leaves are useful in cook-ing. But bay trees may have to be wintered indoors.

The larger, or rather deeper, the soil containers you can provide, the larger trees and shrubs you can grow. Climbing roses such as Etoile de Hollande and the old favourite Caroline Testout both take well to city life. That popular climbing rose Mermaid is not suitable for a roof gar-den, or only for a very large one. It takes up too much space and its spreading branches are too fiercely thorned. Some floribundas have been found to do well in tubs and troughs. Amongst these Alain, Distinction, Golden Delight, and the ever favourite Iceberg flower under city conditions for weeks on end.

With most of his plants and flowers contained in movable pots, the owner of a roof garden can indulge in constant changes of scene. Pots containing flowers that have ceased flowering can be moved to the back, and others, in full bloom, moved forward.

A roof garden is the ideal field for trying gardening experiments. Some plants will succeed for one roof gardener, but may fail for another. But roof gardeners should never be too ambitious. Their aim should be a little garden of their own, suspended between street and sky, which throughout the year will present an ever-changing picture, not neces-sarily of bright colour, but of different greens.

And, a gastronomic postscript . . . for the gourmet who enjoys herbs in his cooking, the sunniest corner of a roof garden is an ideal place for growing pots of thyme, tarragon, and the essential chives.

Garden Furniture

In the museum at Malmaison there is a garden seat which seems—after a century and a half—still to be the ideal in garden furniture. The seat sketched on this page, was made for the use of the fallen Emperor by the ship's carpenter of the Bellerophen, the British man of war which carried him to captivity in remote St. Helena. It is of wood in a simple, yet extremely elegant, design which owes a little to the English taste for Chinoiserie of the late eighteenth century. It could be made by any competent craftsman today. It seems ideal, for its looks, its lightness, its unpretentious design and for, above all, its complete suitability as a piece of garden furniture.

Should garden furniture be of stone, or marble, iron-work or timber?

1, 2 Two views of an exotically planted roof garden on the top floor of a multi-storey London block. Manfred Hermer and Maurice Meyersohn were the architects
3 A garden seat which is a replica of one made for Napoleon's use at St Helena. 'It seems ideal, for its looks, its lightness, its unpretentious design, and, above all, for its complete suitability as a piece of garden furni-ture. . .'
4 Light chairs and table made of painted aluminium in the Chinese Chippendale style designed by Peter Coats and Ian Mylles. The mural is by Martin Newell

3

4

1

As it is the most suitable for so many garden adornments, both useful and decorative, wood seems to be the ideal.

Stone and marble seats are beautiful to look at, but immobile and, in Northern gardens, cold to sit on. In Italy and the South of France, marble seats are warmed by the sun, but in colder climates, marble seldom gets that summer baking which seems to bring out its warm pink and golden tones. Furthermore, in Northern winters, frost is apt to discolour and sometimes crack marble, necessitating the labour of muffling your seats in winter overcoats of straw or sacking. Not for colder climates are marble seats like those in the Pope's garden behind the Vatican where 'in the shady *bosco* fragments of heathen sculpture have been built into garden seats, to aid a cardinal's meditation or lull the siesta of a Legate'.

Stone is more suitable than marble as a material for garden seats in Northern gardens—but that, too, can be cold to sit on unless the seat is protected by some boards or cushions.

2

Iron has its advantages for garden furniture. Chairs and tables of metal can be left out all year round, and can give interest and a lived-in quality to a garden in mid-winter. America excels in the design of light-weight garden seats and chairs in aluminium (as well as in plastic-covered metal or plastic alone, which are much better looking than they sound). In England, recently, there have been experiments in making aluminium chairs and tables in the Chinese Chippendale style. These are elegant, are comparatively light to move about, and look particularly well if painted light tangerine, brunswick green (the blue-green of vine leaves sprayed with copper sulphate), as well as a crisp white.

But wood is the best, the most sympathetic and the most easily worked of all materials for garden furniture. If of oak or natural wood, no material harmonizes so well in a natural setting. And though chairs, seats and tables of soft wood need a preservative coat of paint, a white bench set in a shady corner of the garden offers a very special welcome on warm afternoons.

1 A paved courtyard, its simple lines relieved by plantings of low shrubs, makes a sunlit extension to a large-windowed living-room
2 A garden, on the outskirts of Rome near the Porta San Sebastiano, which is as dramatic as befits its owner, film-actor Marcello Mastroianni. Rugged terracing extends from the wide windows of the *salone* to what were once the walls of the ancient city

1

1 A single jet of water rises from a pool in this slat roofed, sunlit patio
2 A two-level garden in Chelsea in which the upper part (tented and arranged as an outdoor dining-room) is connected with the lower terrace by a spiral staircase. It was designed by Peter Coats and Ian Mylles

The pictures on this page are all of a garden in Ardwick Road, Hampstead where a terrace of York stone and herring-bone brick acts as link between house and garden—as does the flower-bordered terrace shown on the opposite page, in a garden on the Mall at Sheen. On one side is a border of herbaceous plants with a fine clump of delphiniums to the fore. Differently designed pots, some planted with Hydrangeas stand about, giving the sunlit garden a continental air

3

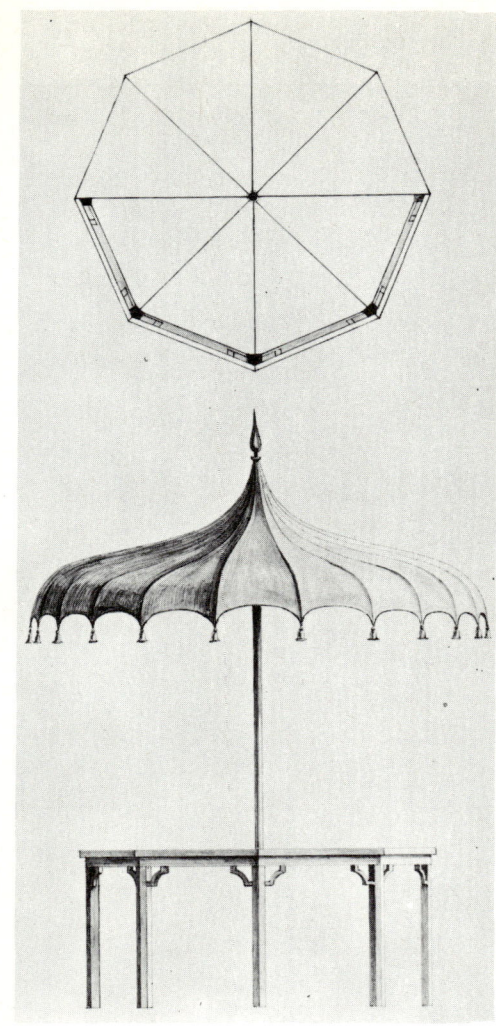

2

3

1 Transatlantic panache in a garden conjured by Otto Zenke with glass-topped table set for four under a hanging baldaquin of blue and white striped sailcloth. The paving is kept clear of planting and is bordered in green box bushes

2 A terrace umbrella (in the 'pagoda' style) and table designed for a Gloucestershire garden by artist Hugh Robson

3 A giant umbrella is a feature of the garden of this Neuilly villa

4 A sun-dappled terrace well-furnished with black and white upholstered chairs and a matching awning. Some shade is essential for every terrace.

4

2

1 A terrace of brick and symmetrical paving stones is sheltered by the old walls of Ince Castle, and dressed with well-established wistaria and magnolia

2 A garden seat of stone, cushioned with living thyme, devised by that great gardener the Hon. Victoria Sackville-West, in the herb garden at Sissinghurst Castle, in Kent

3 A garden seat on wheels, said once to have been used by Queen Victoria at Osborne, in a garden at Hampstead

4 'Not for colder climates are marble seats like those in the Pope's garden behind the Vatican where, in the shady *bosco* fragments of heathen sculpture have been built into garden seats, to aid a cardinal's meditation or lull the siesta of a legate'

1, 2

3

4

1 Paving, a snake-legged seat, and the aromatic foliage of balm (Melissa officinalis) at The Ring, near Saffron Walden in Essex

2 A garden bench in the German garden of Veitshöchheim which seems to be the epitome of Rococo elegance.

3 Easily moved furniture in white wire-work in a London garden. The circular paved area makes sitting out possible in all but the wettest weather. Overhead, a fine Magnolia grandiflora.

4 Terracing as fine as a carpet is a feature of this garden between Creil and Clermont. The grey and mauve tones of the old setts are laid in a petal-like pattern designed by the landscape gardener, René Péchère

1 The groundwork of this garden in Earl's Court is of random set stone with the joints closely cemented to prevent weeds. A surprising variety of plants can be successfully grown in the heart of London

2 Baroque railings and a presiding bust in Camberwell

3 Bay trees and Spanish trellis in Chelsea

4 Victoriana, green grass and a paved area for dining

5 This terrace in Winchester centres on a built-up rainwater tank. In the foreground (left) is a spreading plant of Santolina viridis

3, 4   5

1

1, 2 A group of enterprising young British architects, Garnett, Cloughley, Blakemore and Associates, devised this paved terrace sunk into a Chiltern hillside. The roof of the broad-eaved house (a series of pavilions) is covered with silvery cedarwood shingles, and the whole terrace is an example of the striking effect of a one-colour scheme

3 Greenery softens the glare, and a Japanese parasol provides shade for this snug terrace by a garden pool

4 A pool with built-up sides for cushions and sitting out in a small London garden

3

4

1 A design for a small Chelsea garden in trelliswork with a raised platform and false perspective to give a feeling of space. This sort of garden looks well even in winter

2 Six old pillars supporting a balustrade of ornamental woodwork give quality to a small town garden. Both drawings by Hugh Robson after designs by Peter Coats

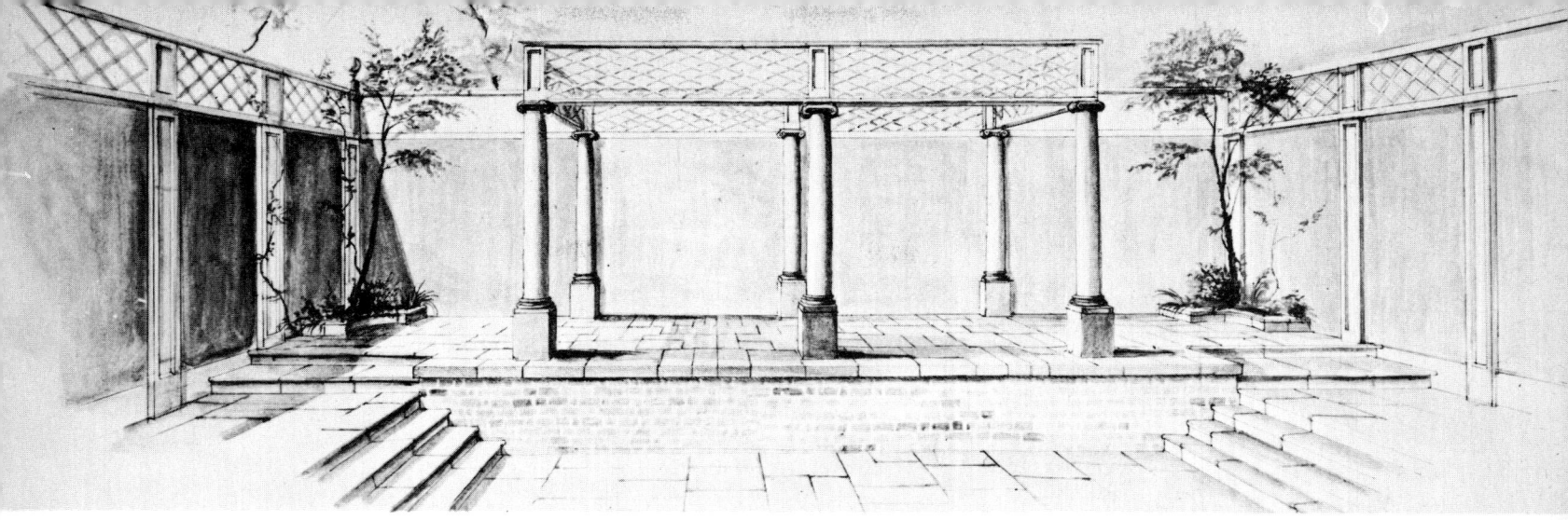

2

3 A terrace and steps bordered with white petunias, behind a mews house in Mayfair. The decorative *lunette* panels over the windows are described on page 190

4 A terrace of random paving with a giant Yucca gloriosa and brooding Buddha as genius loci. Change of level is an advantage in the smallest garden

4

1 Chairs and a table of simple form in the topiary garden at Haseley Court in Oxfordshire
2 At Crowhill on Farnham Common in Buckinghamshire—a tree is made the centre point of garden living and is encircled with a seat. In the foreground, an ivy draped bust
3 A slenderly pillared and porticoed terrace overlooks a garden of young spring foliage and blossom. A house at Grand Rapids, Michigan, designed in Southern Colonial style by John Volk and Warren Rindge

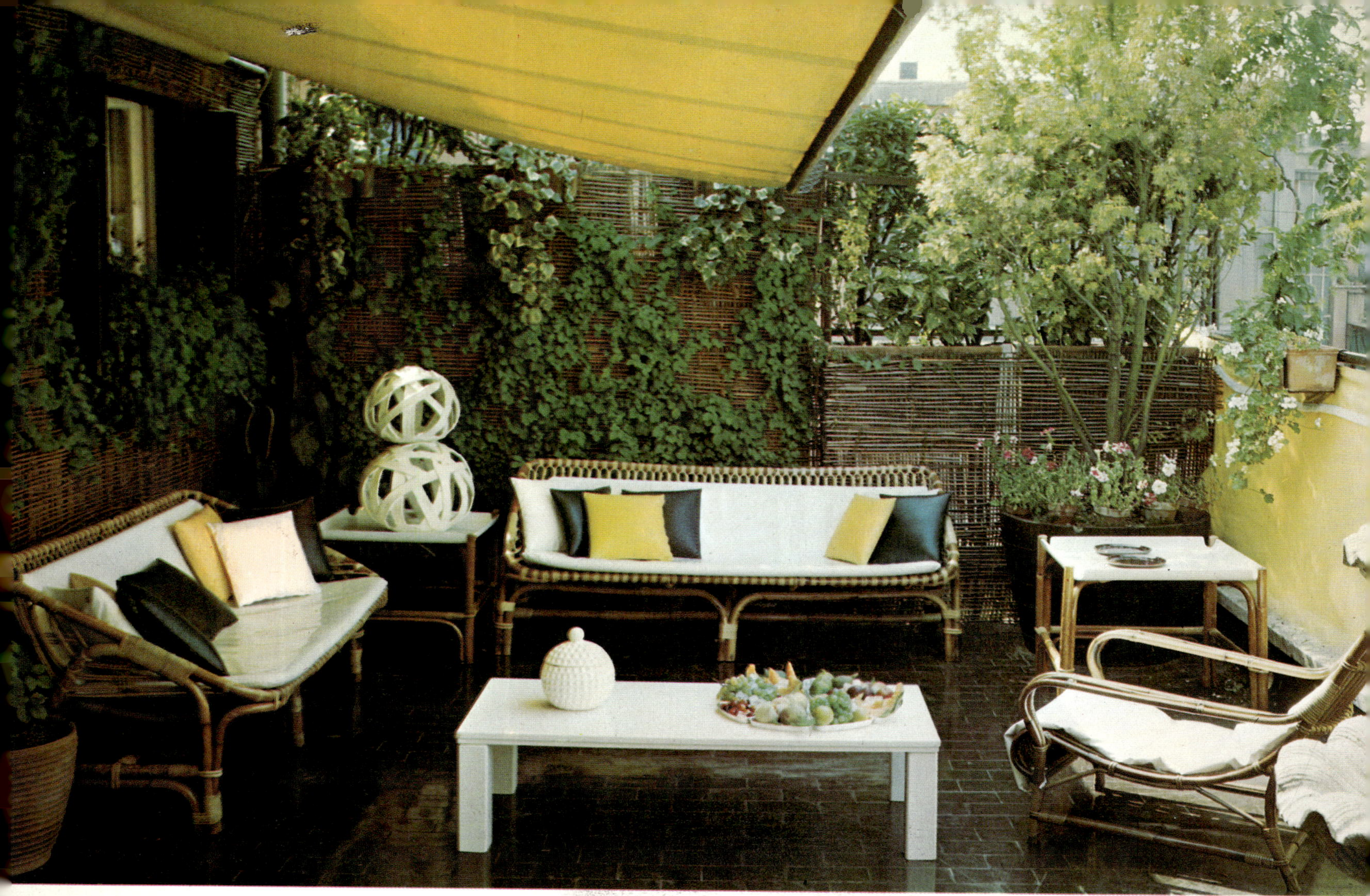

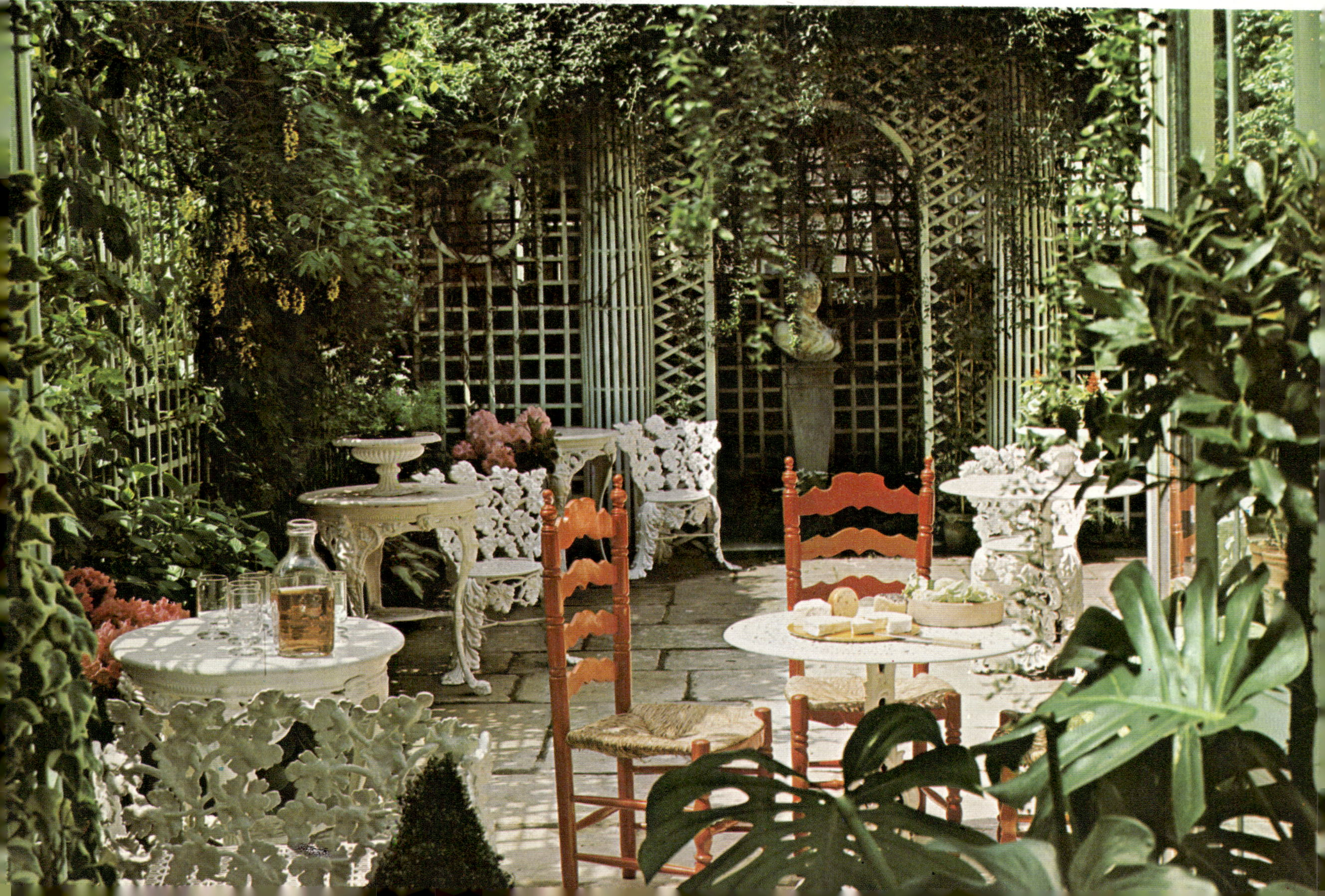

1 This terrace in Rome has a riverside look with its screens of reed hung with different coloured ivies. The light leaved tree is Acer negundo

2 The enclosed garden of a house in Islington, with architecturally trellised walls, and coral-painted Victorian ironwork furniture, makes a cool retreat on summer days

3 A modern version of pergola, in white painted timber, provides broken shade in a Kensington garden designed by John Brookes

4 The loggia of architect Paul Quintrand's house at Aix en Provence is roofed with panels of split cane. Movable louvres give protection, when necessary, from the sun

1 White painted furniture of elaborate ironwork in a corner of a London garden. The bench has a seat of wood, which is warmer and more comfortable for sitting on than iron

2 Grouped around a marble-topped table which once was in a Public House; a Victorian cast iron bench and modern aluminium chairs provide an inviting sitting-out place

3 Reproduction Victorian garden seat in the well known but always attractive Fernleaf design

4 Victorian spring-bottom chairs on a magnolia flanked terrace in Hampshire. Beyond, steps lead up to a beech shaded lawn

5 A well-furnished loggia, curtained with creepers and pleasingly set out with furniture, opens off a house in Tangier. The hanging light is concealed by a Moroccan bird cage

1 In this terraced garden in St John's Wood—brick walling, symmetrical paving, gravel and bold plantings of evergreens make a pleasing outdoor décor all year round

2 White wire chairs on a roofed-in garden on the top of a high new block in Victoria. Draped in greenery is a relief in Lasa marble by the Hungarian sculptor Erno Szegedi.

3, 4 A module which can be used for many purposes. David Millet designed the block module out of which can be conjured walls, seats, free standing sculptural objects, tables —and so on—to furnish or embellish the garden as desired.

5 Chairs and table in reinforced concrete offer sculptural decoration as well as a sitting out place. Made in assymetrical blocks, they can be used in many different ways.

6 An ivy-walled terrace in Paris of which all the furniture and plant containers are of glistening white polyester. The chairs, with their easily removable cushion-coverings are designed by Paulin for Artifort; the sofa of polyester, reinforced with fibre-glass, is by Whilkan

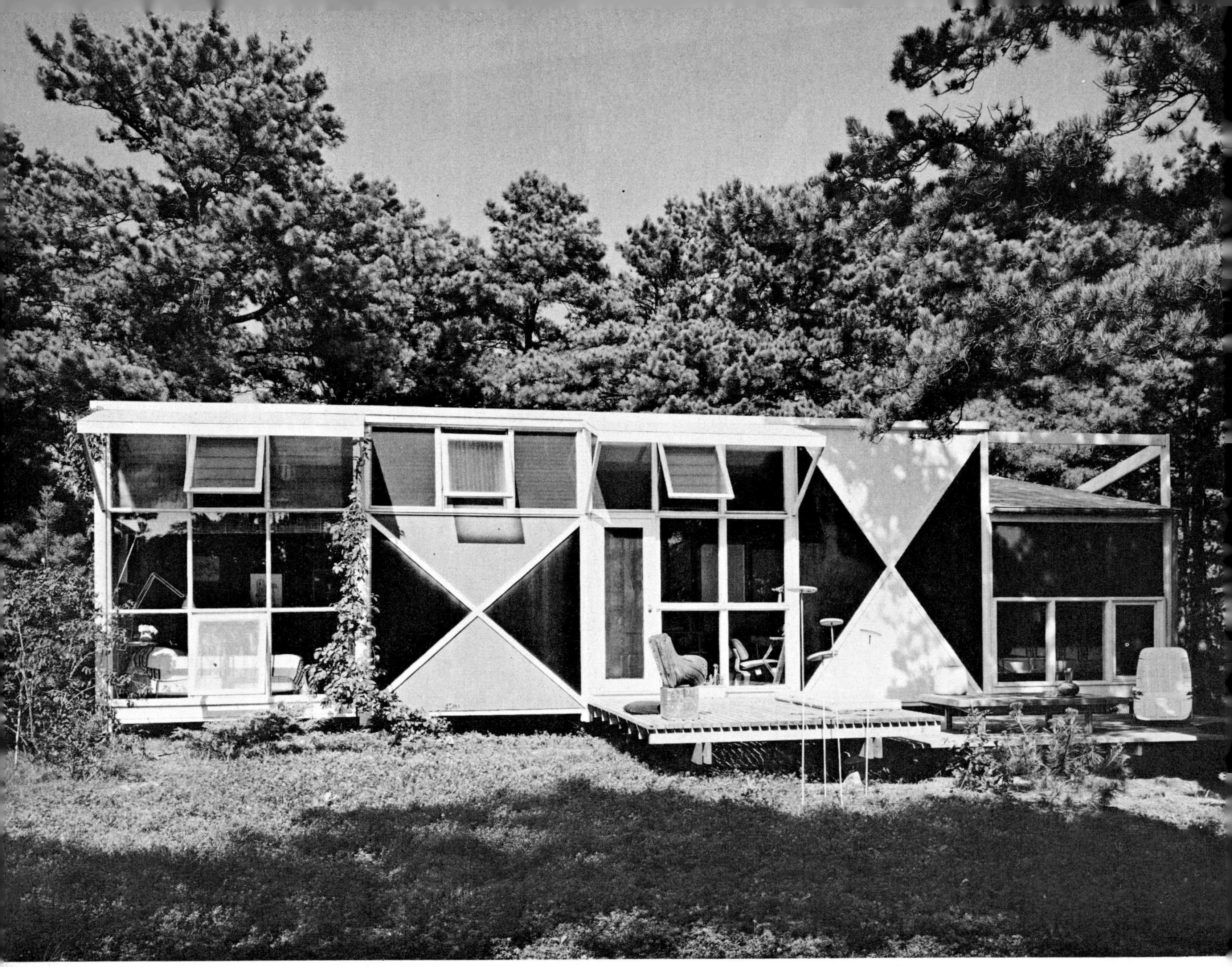

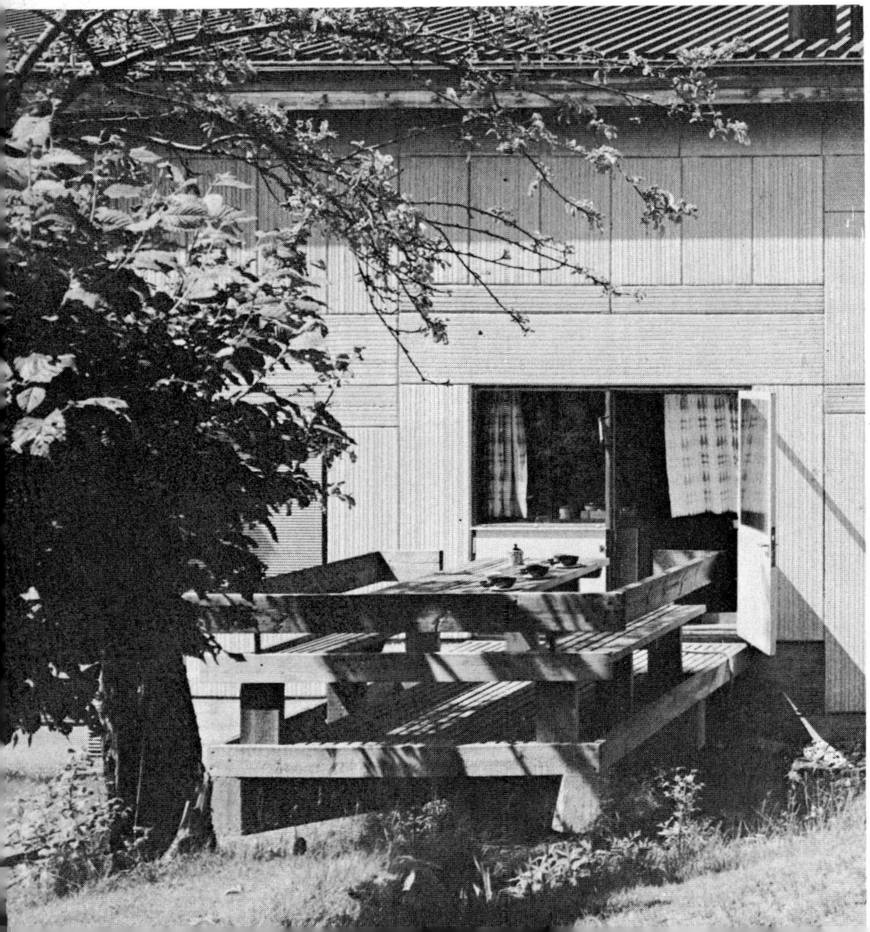

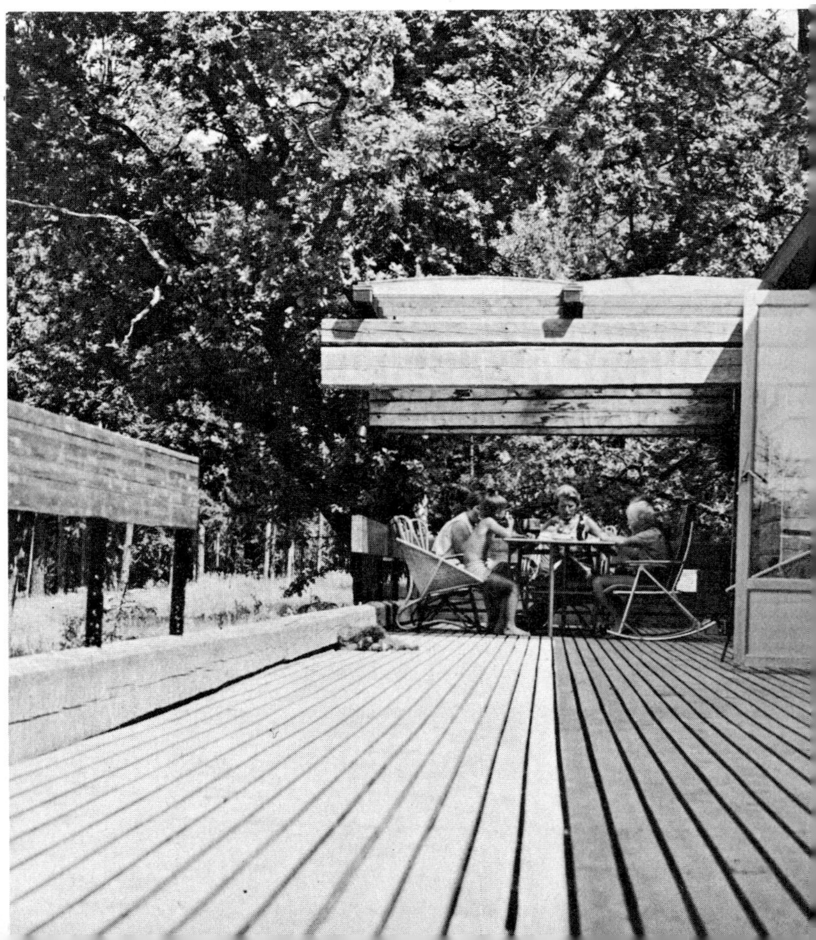

4

1 This eye-catching façade belongs to a cottage at Cape Cod, Massachusetts. The wall panels with their 'bow-tie' bracing are in red and white, and yellow and blue. The terrace is of wooden decking and the architect/owner is the celebrated British architect, Serge Chermayeff, since 1962 Professor of Architecture at Yale

2 A well-known British architect Ralph Erskine devised this breakfast terrace complete with seats and table opening off the kitchen of his house near Dröttningholm in Sweden

3 In Sweden, sun-decks made of well weathered cedar are often used instead of the more conventional terracework of stone

4 Changes of levels, always valuable in a small garden, create a strong pattern of light and shade behind American architect Nathan Silver's house in Cambridge

, 3

1 A pattern of light and shade cast by a classic pergola of slats. No fussy planting has been allowed to detract from the fine wood-work

2 In this American garden a slatted and glassed-in roof shelters a gravel terrace effectively paved with giant stepping stones of slate

3 Green and white for a cool Atrium. Chairs ideal for sunbathing stand about, while unwelcome breezes are excluded by a glass roof overhead. The large-leaved plant, itself like a green sculpture, is a monstera

4 A terrace floor of wooden planks in a draughtsboard design, with simple squared-off upright posts, recalls Japan, though the view beyond is of the Bay of Arcachon

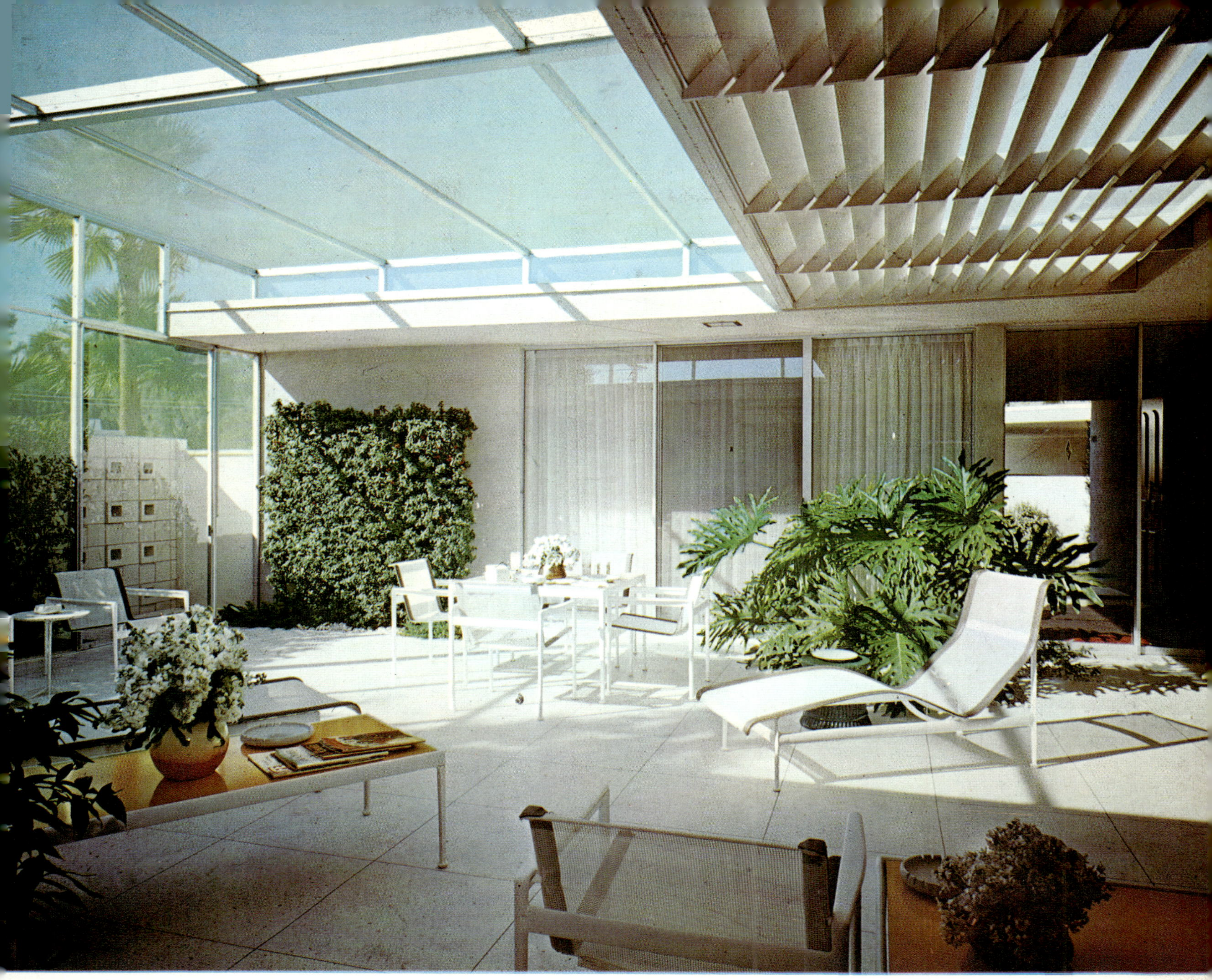
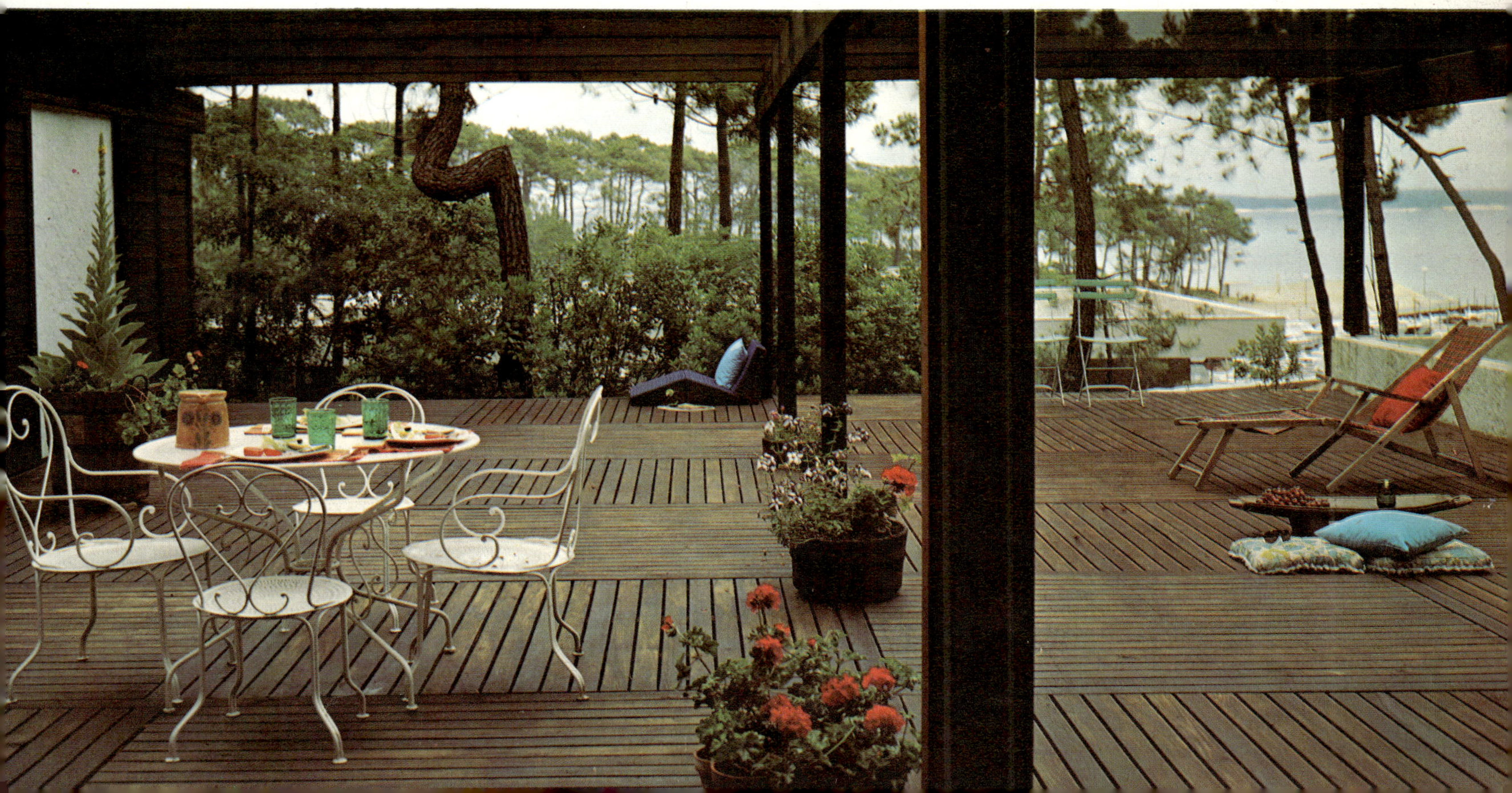

STEPS, PATHS AND PERGOLAS

make the stairs, passages and corridors of the well-ordered garden

As a staircase is to a home, so a flight of steps is to a garden. Not only are garden steps sometimes necessary, owing to the lie of the land, but it is often desirable in flat and featureless gardens to create a change in levels, and link them with steps of stone or brick.

The flight of steps in the gardens at Versailles is one of the wonders of garden architecture, and all the great gardens of Italy boast moss-grown (and sometimes hazardous) steps from terrace to terrace. And in our own smaller gardens, juggling with different levels can be a subtle and fascinating exercise. Despite all the loving care in the world, a flat garden runs the risk of becoming boring. A difference in level of only two feet in a small town garden can make it look bigger, provided that the steps joining the two levels melt into the scene. The walker should be able to go from level to level without really noticing the rise or fall. If a great many steps are unavoidable, there should never be more than a dozen steps together, and each group should be divided by a landing. Dramatic flights of garden stairs, as in the garden of Glenveagh Castle, right, need a more grandiose setting than most gardeners can provide.

The most natural material to use for steps is the local stone, and fortunate are garden-makers in, say, the English Cotswold country, where unlimited natural supplies are there to hand. But any solid quarry stone, preferably rough in texture, can be used for the purpose. A fairly thick slab can serve as the step, or several slabs jointed together, with the risers supporting these made of several chunks of rock. Experienced gardeners lay their stones and mortar on a light foundation of bitumen; and the same method is used for brick steps. Wood, which

1 A flight of grass steps in a garden near Septeuil, of which the risers are of moss-grown, rounded bricks. The steps lead from an area of lawn to a wilder part of the garden, and are balustraded with cotoneaster
2 A spectacular flight of steps leads upwards through the trees in the garden of Glenveagh Castle, Co. Donegal

is often used because it weathers so well, can either take the form of planks, or better still of trunks or half-trunks secured at the edges by two pegs. It is a good idea to slope the steps slightly so as to avoid water stagnation.

As everybody knows, the shortest distance between two points is a straight line. However, this principle is not evident in nature and should be studiously avoided for garden steps. Ideally the flight should sweep in a curve to follow the contour of the ground. One can place three or four steps together and then scatter the rest; one can also build the steps in unequal widths and, at the landing, continue the flight on up the slope on a different axis. For a flight of steps which is rather formal, an atmosphere of movement can be achieved by making the planting spill over the stairs on one side or the other.

The junction of the path and steps should be studied with care; if the steps lead onto the path and are also the only means of exit from it, one must decide which of the two is to be the wider. Wide steps are always attractive, but to narrow them slightly can make the walker pause, if it is intended to attract his attention to a particular point in the garden. There again, there is something to be said for 'breaking' the axis of the path and steps. It is not a good idea to put the path at right angles to the steps; this makes too sharp a turn, and all sharp, unnatural turns in a garden are undesirable. A happier effect can be achieved by making the one fork off the other in the direction of the most frequented part of the garden.

1 Well-laid paving of York stone below the balconied façade of a Hampstead house
2 Brick and dressed stone, in perfect proportion, pave the way between lines of lime trees at Alderley Grange in Gloucestershire

Paths

Paths have been well described as the vertebrae of the garden, the bones of its design. For some, grass paths will always be the ideal, though gardeners of experience prefer paved paths and, in very big gardens, gravelled ones, for the pleasing contrast they make with areas of verdure or flowers; for one must never forget that paths have an important role to play: that of 'proclaiming the style of the garden'. Paths can be given importance by being kept simple, be made mysterious by unexpected curves and bends, amusing by the material used and the fantasy in design, or be made an integral part of the garden by having creeping plants planted between the slabs.

Obviously there must be a certain harmony between the character of the garden and the paths laid down. Old cobblestones are charming, strewn in an informal garden, but are not for a formal garden. Nor do perfectly carved paving stones look at home in a rock garden.

Materials for paths now available offer a large variety of finish, cut and colour. In very small gardens, stone paths often give way to 'Japanese stepping stones' which are sunk into the lawn. These have one great advantage in that they do not spoil the general line of the lawn when it is looked at as a whole, and if they are set low enough,

1

do not interfere with mowing.

Natural stone paving looks right and is long-lasting, but the garden-maker's first problem is to find rocks which are neither slippery nor liable to split. The criteria for one's choice are not necessarily physical, for the quality of the stone is very important and each one has a different finish to it. Simply hewn rocks look well in any garden, for they can be cut either geometrically or haphazardly and still look perfectly natural.

The use of pebbles is always successful for paths which are meant to

2

give pleasure to the eye rather than the feet, but pebbles should be graded, and then laid on a smooth concrete surface. The kind of cobbled paving sometimes seen in French gardens, in a shell pattern, can also look effective—as shown on page 80 (no. 3).

In laying slabs of stone, holes should be dug for them and lined with sand; the sand stabilizes them and prevents them from sinking. If the paving is to be pointed, then a mixture of cement and sand should be laid on top, brushed in, and then watered. If the paving is to be planted, the crevices between should be filled with compost.

1 Bricks laid demurely two by two in a basket work pattern makes a path in the white garden at Sissing-hurst Castle. On either side, silver leaved Santolina chamaecypa rissus
2 Old faded bricks make perfect paths for cottage gardens. On either side of this one grow herbaceous plants, and to the left is a fine clump of Cineraria maritima

71

2

Recently, enterprising gardeners have used wood to make original looking paths. These consist of round slices of hard wood, such as oak or walnut: but they should be treated with fungicides before being put into place. They are laid on a bed of sand or gravel. Page 80 (no. 2).

But there are endless different kinds of paths to choose, just as in a house there are endless floor coverings for passages. Working paths, which have to bear constant treading or the passage of wheelbarrows and garden machinery, must, of course, be tougher than paths designed for the occasional garden visitors. Gravel paths are more practical under trees, squares of cement set deep in turf make mowing easy. And in an enclosed rose-garden, or a herb garden like the beautiful one at Sissinghurst Castle in Kent, there can be few more pleasing paths than those of thyme-grown paving stones which outline the beds of tarragon and mint. Page 81 (no. 8).

Pergolas

For gardens in the south a pergola provides an extension to the house, as well as an opportunity for original and interesting planting.

The very word pergola makes one think of marble columns seen in Venice and Tuscany, or the old peasant shelters made from lattice that one sees by Lake Como. Pergolas are walks built to provide half-shade, vine-grown trellises which filter the sun's rays, or light shelters in dappled sunlight in which to sit and rest. But for the last half-century, gardeners have lost interest in pergolas, though now they are coming back into favour. In fact the terrace, that 'outdoor room' between house and garden, often needs some kind of cover which assures some shade. As it protects the terrace or is extended to cover a path, the

1 Twin paths, with a riband of flowers between, under a rose covered trellis in a garden in Tripoli
2 A path under a leafy tunnel of arching limes in the Baroque garden of the Residenz at Würzburg

1

1 A giant star in close-set pebbles in the famous Boboli Gardens in Florence
2 Bricks singly and in pairs make a narrow passage between shrub roses at Alderley Grange in Gloucestershire. The Damask rose to the left is Isfahan

pergola can provide planting space for many plants which, because they are climbers, are difficult to find a place for in the garden and which, grown on a pergola, now prove their worth as well as looking beautiful.

Before decorating them, pergolas must first be built, and they must be built in harmony with the style of the house. With a contemporary style they should be slim and elegant, but with a period house they must not look too new. They can be unsightly if painted too staringly in white. If you want your pergola to be rustic, it must be genuine and you should use young trees in their natural state or beams squared with an axe, not rawly sawn and planed. For the bases, old weathered bricks should be used.

It is relatively easy to find plants to cover the vertical supports of a pergola; it is less so for the horizontal beams. Covering the pergola with a narrowly-spaced lattice runs the risk of turning it into a dark tunnel. An openwork one with a large mesh is easier, but can be ugly. If you are a handyman yourself, or have someone who is, you can cover the top of your pergola with nylon netting which is invisible two yards away. When choosing plants, care should be taken not to have plants which will blossom only on top of the pergola, so that the flowers can only be seen by passing birds. It is better to grow two separate kinds of plants; some which will flower on the supports and some which will spread along the roof.

There are many plants which can be used to deck the well-dressed pergola. Roses, clematis, the purple leaved vines and wistaria are almost too obvious to mention. Solanum crispum, the climbing potato, jasmine, Actinidia chinensis, passiflora—the Passion Flower—and for impatient gardeners, the quick growing annual Cobaea scandens, with its greenish purple bells, are less obvious pergola-plants which will quickly reach a height of eight feet or more.

2

1 The 'Jardin De Curé' at its best—
with its box bordered path of old
highway paving stones set in gravel
2 Oblong paving blocks of cement
make an attractive pattern under a
wistaria-dressed pergola. Being set
deep in grass the blocks do not
impede the work of the lawn mower
3 Lilium regale line a pergola-shaded
path in a London garden only a few
miles from Hyde Park Corner

3

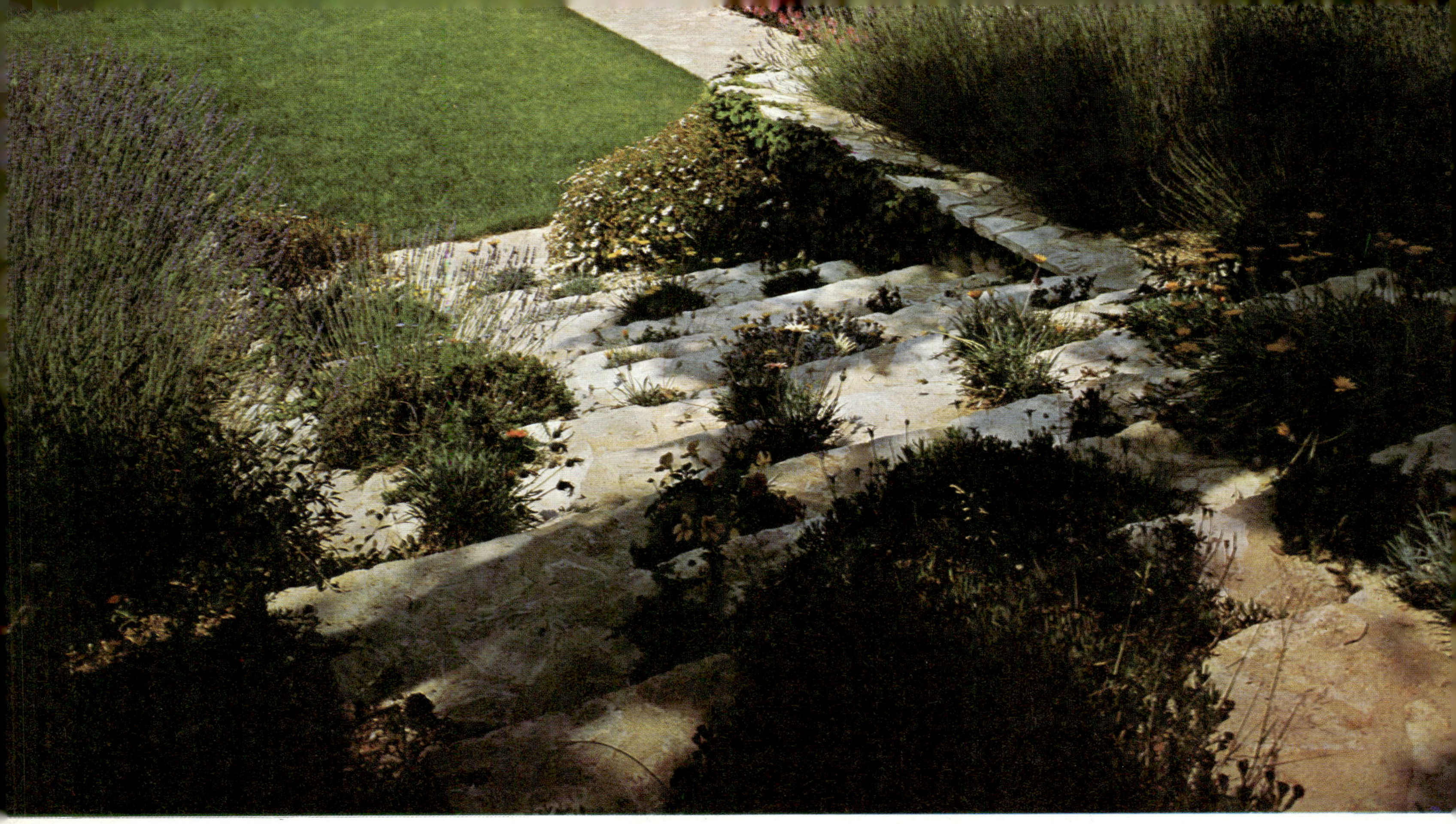

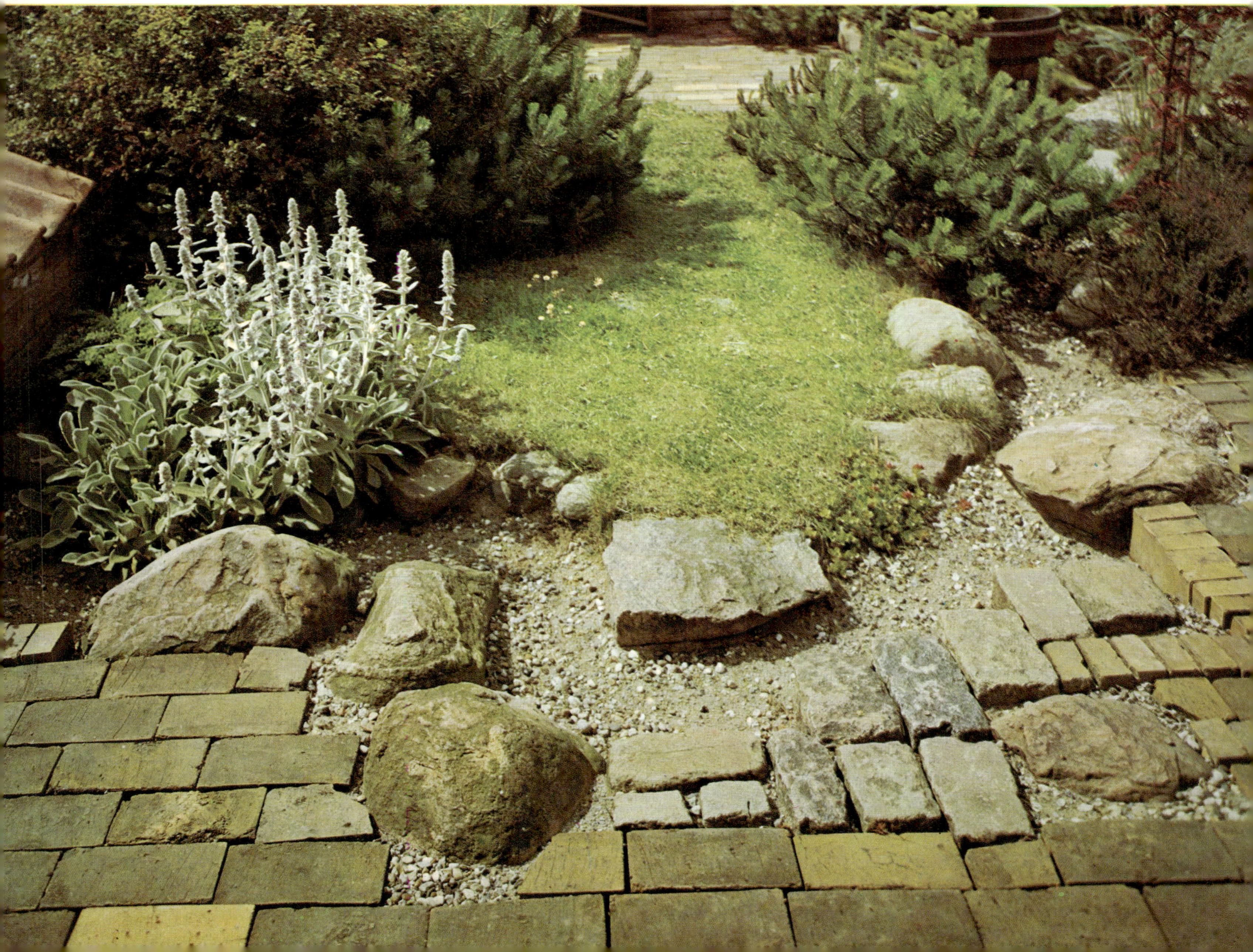

1 In this sheltered courtyard of a villa near St Tropez a lawn shows its fresh green in a framework of white paved paths. It is approached by shallow steps in which lavender and potentillas have been allowed to seed themselves

2 Gravel, edged with bricks and small boulders, makes a cool grey and green corner in a Danish garden. The plants—low conifers and silver Stachys lanata—were chosen for their soft colouring and permanent effect.

3 A chequer-board design of concrete blocks and turf in a setting of roses and large leaved hostas, in a garden in Chelsea

4 Paving stones set deep in turf for ease of mowing make an informal path for a cottage near Rambouillet

1

2

1 Squares of old paving setts and blocks of concrete make a pleasing pattern

2 Unusual groundwork of circular tree trunks sawn flat, and laid in concrete. More tree trunks provide simple seats and a rustic balustrade

3 Paving in a radiating petal pattern, designed by René Péchère, makes the groundwork of this courtyard of a small country house near Paris

4 Bold roundels of an aggregate of pebbles and cement; a path made by digging out round shallow holes and pouring in the 'mixture'

5 There is no end to the decorative use of well-planted pots which can act as punctuation marks in the well-furnished garden

6 Old paving setts with grass growing between them look attractive, but present a maintenance problem

3

4

5

6

7

8

9

10

7 Paving laid in a decorative pattern combining cobbles, bricks and old paving stones. The presiding plants are a variegated aloe and Sisyrinchium striatum

8 Thyme grown stones make the paths in the herb garden at Sissinghurst Castle

9 Cobbles, closely set in a giant diamond pattern in brick, provide a subtle contrast of colour and texture

10 A path of zig-zag tiles of brilliant blue and white in an enclosed patio garden in Marrakesh. It acts as a perfect foil for luxurious foliage

11 A swagged urn and neat paving of sexagonal tiles in a garden in France

12 An original path of concrete blocks bearing the impressions of exotic leaves such as palmettos, at the Villa La Leonina, Beaulieu, Alpes Maritimes

11

12

4

1 Prefabricated slabs of sea-washed pebbles set in concrete make a beautifully textured path in the flower garden of Ince Castle in Cornwall
2 Concrete and cobble-work squares laid in a diamond pattern and set deep in turf to facilitate mowing
3 Prefabricated blocks of concrete and cobble-work make a checkerboard path bordered to the right with a carpet of ground covering, weed suppressing ivy
4 Tesselated paving in a bold design by the swimming-pool in the garden of a villa at Neuilly
5 Closely-set cobbles make a classical looking path, pretty to see, but impractical for high heels

1 Outsize panels of concrete set in cobbles and cement and gravel make neat, weed-free going in a courtyard of cool white brick

2 Concrete blocks in strictest symmetry, laid in gravel, make a practical path for a modern building

3 Paving stones set in loose pebbles provide a pleasing path for the courtyard of a house built less than ten years ago

4 Informally laid blocks between pleached limes in the spring garden at Sissinghurst Castle in Kent

5 Formally laid concrete blocks between brimming borders in a garden in Winchester. The plant to the left is steely blue-leaved eryngium

4

,3   5

2

1 A winding path suggests that this London garden is far larger than it is. Behind the stone seat, a shrubby veronica

2 Gravel paths retained by stone setts in the rock garden at Wakehurst in Sussex. For gravel paths such as these a warm colour should be chosen. Cold grey granite chippings or staring white gravel are quite unsuitable

3 A curving gravel path, stone edged for tidiness, sweeps round a fine clump of paeonies in the garden at Pusey, near Faringdon in Berkshire

1

3

1 A path over-canopied with a pergola of roses in the famous rose garden in Madrid, the Rosaleda

2 A circular plat of cobbles and brick makes a path junction in a garden laid out in the French taste in the Isle of Wight. Beyond, *arcures* of roses and vines

3 An apple-tunnel, planned many years ago, throws dappled shadows on a gravel path in the garden at Tyninghame Castle in Scotland

4 In this foliage-filled London area the plain path of old paving stones is bordered with rope-edged tiles

5 A tessellated path under a vine-grown pergola leads to a Baroque fountain in pebble work in the great German garden of Schloss Mainau on the shores of Lake Constance

1   4

1 Low steps of York stone lead from a lawn to a slightly raised terrace

2 Five steps in an unusual combination of sand and stone lead gently to an upper lawn

3 Steps should be planned broad enough to take the foot like these

4 Steps in a woodland setting with risers of slender tree trunks and steps of grass. Long-lasting hard wood is best for steps like these

5 In the corner of this garden in Hampshire are well-proportioned steps in brick. To the left and right grow two excellent 'furnishing' plants, Cotoneaster horizontalis and Vitis coignetiae

2, 3   5

1 There are few forms of steps so graceful and inviting as a semi–circular flight in brick set on edge. Burford House, Tenbury Wells in Worcestershire

2 The well–known Italian garden designer Pietro Porcenai created these poetically curving steps of stone set in verdure

3 These elaborate steps surfaced in black and white pebbles from the nearby beach at Bray are in the Powerscourt demesne, one of Ireland's greatest gardens

4 Twin flights of curved steps in carved stone lead to an *allée* of soaring cypresses in H.M. The Queen Mother of Roumania's garden at the Villa Sparta in Florence

2, 3   4

2

1 Iron steps with railing in different forms and patterns give interest to a paved Chelsea garden

2 Rock-garden steps, as long as they provide comfortable passage, can be luxuriantly overgrown. Here sempervivum and dwarf helichrysum have nearly, but not quite, taken over

3 Wood is a material which could be more often employed for garden steps—especially in town gardens; but as wooden steps can be slippery they are best provided with hand rails, as here

4 Steps to a seldom-used door make a stand for pots and stone vases of many coloured flowers, such as pelargoniums, geraniums and grey-leaved echeverias at Folkington Place in Sussex

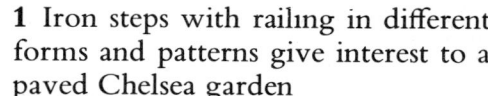

SUMMER HOUSES

Pavilions, follies, gazebos or loggias offer places of relaxation in the open air

One of the more curious and perverse of the Northern gardener's many quirks, and that least understandable to Mediterranean gardeners, is their preoccupation with shelters, summer-houses, loggias and so forth. They could understand quite readily if these structures were made for keeping off the rain, but when they hear that they are for shade, they smile, shake their heads and continue with their perambulations.

Why anyone with a pleasant house and a pleasant garden should then wish to build another, smaller, incommodious, temporary, useless house in the garden, is a question only to be answered by a psychiatrist specializing in the more decorative manias of mankind.

Yet there it is. House-owners, landscape gardeners, architects, plain and ordinary potterers-about-the-garden, and almost anyone with more than a quarter of an acre of their own commission, wants a folly, a gazebo, call it what you will. Summer-house is the most usually used word, a shelter from the midday sun, as if we had learned one lesson from those faded sepia pictures of our grandmothers venturing into the garden in wide-brimmed hats, as if the sun of Sicily or Luxor were beating down upon their pompadours.

The fact remains: give any gardener the chance to build a summer-house or other shady conceit, and he is off to his graph paper straight away: in spite of one important snag.

Nowadays, these oddities of architectural self-expression seem to have to be justified, for this is the Utilitarian Age when conspicuous consumption may only be practised by governments, and not by individuals. In the eighteenth century there was less hypocrisy about self-indulgence, self-expression and the rest of the more harmless examples of man's humanity to man. If a man felt like having a house, folly, ruin or grotto in his garden he could go ahead. Nowadays Pope wouldn't have stood a chance to build that grotto in his Twickenham garden which became so famous, and the prototype of many others.

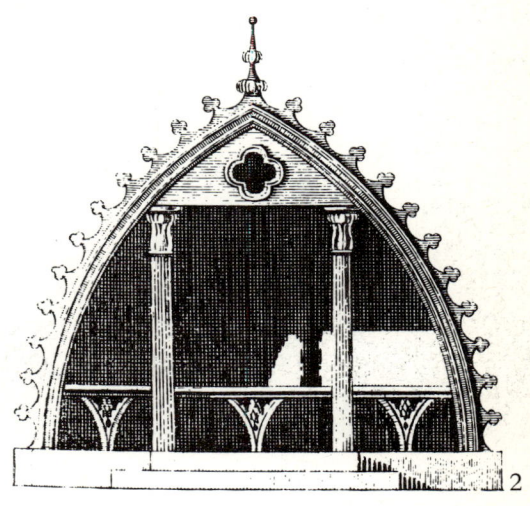

1 A pool-house with a Moroccan look at Pylewell Park in Hampshire. It was designed by architect Harry Graham
2 The drawing, as the others are in this section, is from an early nineteenth century Franco-German publication *Phantasien* or the *Petit Magasin ou Receuil d'idées d'une execution peu dispensieuse*, by the publisher and professor of philosophy J. G. Grohmann of Leipzig

For most of us the loggia surely is the perfect compromise. If we have fifty acres to play with and a convenient knoll from which to survey our pleasaunce, a well-placed shade-giving gazebo is a practical and decorative element in the whole design. But for many the real pleasure of a garden is to survey it from the back door. The narrowest plot, with thought, can be given an impression of modest infinity. Darker trees encompass our domain. Skilful planting has eradicated all indication of where our neighbour's plot begins and ends. We are at one with our own creation. What better place than a place of semi-shade, semi-indolence, semi-stirrings of conscience (shouldn't I be out there doing some pruning?), in fact, semi-everything apart from one hundred per cent visual pleasure? The gardener neglects the pleasure offered by a loggia at the expense of hours of additional gardening delight. There he can have his meals in peace, defiant of all but a tropical gale; there he can reflect upon next spring's major garden developments; there he can write his letters, keep his accounts and, on what was once called the Day of Rest, keep himself up to date with the overloaded world of the Sunday press.

In his day a man could build his retreat in any architectural manner that took his fancy. An eighteenth-century gardener suddenly caught into the pleasures of 'landskip' design could borrow his motifs from Stonehenge, Venice or Wilton. He could commission lattice-work in beech, or iron-work; he could make his finials in obelisk or pineapple form; he could insist upon the columns of his loggia being of the Corinthian or Tuscan order of the day, and nobody would raise an eyebrow. As far as the garden was concerned eclecticism was acceptable. But not today. No sooner than you decide on a gazebo in the Hindu taste, inspired by the temples and kiosks of Sezincote, than the Local Council will be down on you like (or with) a ton of bricks, if they'd heard you were planning any such extravagance.

Fortunate Pope! Although he may have spurned the upstart, Batty Langley, he no doubt sifted the advice of his many friends, for no circle of acquaintances has ever been more prodigal with suggestions.

But Langley had his points. Although so frantically and gothically inventive, many of his suggestions for garden pavilions and temples had a considerable decorative charm.

For the felicities of garden folly architecture, even Langley must be placed a long way behind the indefatigable, early nineteenth-century enthusiast for garden adornment, M. Boitard of Paris, who published a classic work, *L'Art de Composer et Décorer les Jardins*. M. Boitard's book contains the most light-hearted, as well as practical, ideas for temples, follies, birdcages, bee-houses, dovecotes, swings, roundabouts, water-wheels and even tombs. Many of his designs would be a joy to any garden owner of today, however large or small his domain.

M. Boitard's fantasies may seem a trifle elaborate for the suburban

This Orientally inspired gazebo with its pagoda roof, which was first shown at the Paris Exhibition of 1869, has for years decorated the water garden at Cliveden in Buckinghamshire

1 The graceful Pin Mill building, dating from 1730, overlooks a canal-shaped lily pond in the famous garden at Bodnant in North Wales. It was rescued, in a derelict state, from Gloucestershire, before the war
2 A conical pavilion, shell house below and dovecote above, by the lily pond at Ince Castle in Cornwall

gardener. Yet one wonders. In much the same way that a writer, in some recent book on fruit-growing in the small garden, contends that peaches can be grown in a town back garden, ideas can be borrowed from these rather grand notions and adapted to quite modest gardens. An arch, or trompe l'oeil arch, can give a new look to any wall; lattice-work can add distinction to the façade of any loggia (see page 116); so, too, can columns, which don't have to be great stone columns from some once-vast, but now demolished, *porte-cochère* but can be cut to the right length or height from cast-iron piping that your builder uses for drainage, or can be cast in fibre-glass. The ideas are there all right.

Nowadays, certainly, we are less fanciful than our forefathers. When we want a garden house, a loggia or just a shed we invariably seek one of the multitudinous designs that our enterprising wood-working specialist houses have produced, send a cheque and back comes a huge, skilfully-packaged load of prefabricated timber and glass. All we have to do is to assemble it, usually with little more trouble than a modest display of muscle, and the insertion of a dozen strategically placed nuts and bolts.

1 A loggia in the Italianate style, with pillars, in the garden at Nymans in Sussex, one of the most celebrated gardens in England, famous for its camellias and magnolias

2 This Oriental aviary was designed by Lord Snowdon and makes the centre point of a garden of herbaceous plants at Mereworth Castle in Kent

3 A kiosk in Oriental style is a recent addition to the grounds of Sezincote in Gloucestershire. It overlooks the tennis court

1 In the famous palm garden of La Palmeraie in Marrakesh is this simple, yet supremely elegant, retreat. The garden was laid out by the well-known French artist Majorelle

2 Eight slender pillars hold aloft a canopy of glass over a fountain in a Moroccan garden. The groundwork is of blue and white zig-zag tiles

3 A tented shelter held aloft by Roman spears overlooks this swimming pool on a hillside near Cannes in the South of France

![Trellis-work summer house in a garden setting]

1 A garden pavilion in brick with an ogival, pineapple-crowned roof in the garden at Hidcote in Gloucestershire
2 Garden house at Ampthill in Bedfordshire, home of the late Sir Albert Richardson
3 A summer house in brightly painted *tôle* which would not have looked out of place at the Field of Cloth of Gold, or the Eglinton Tournament
4 The trellis-work summer house, in a setting of hornbeam hedges at King Henry's Hunting Lodge near Odiham in Hampshire. It was designed by the celebrated interior decorator, John Fowler
5 Flora protected from the keener breezes of the Firth of Forth by a pavilion of trellis work. Her shelter, though it looks typical of the eighteenth century, was added to the garden at Tyninghame less than three years ago

1 In the garden of the Villa Ivanovic at Formentor in Majorca there is this curtained pavilion, which makes an outdoor dining-room
2 The Rotunda at Stowe in Buckinghamshire, where it has stood in solitary grandeur since Sir John Vanbrugh designed it in 1719

1 A garden house with an ogival roof is seen over flower-beds at Claverton Manor, the American Museum, near Bath. It is modelled on George Washington's miniature school house at Mount Vernon, in which he gave his step-grandchildren their lessons

2 White lattice, as a material for garden structure, has a lightness and suitability unmatched by any other material. A gazebo with a graceful roof at Oyster Bay, U.S.A.

3 A simple summer house of classical form, but made of rustic wood

4 A garden house, screened with panels of trellis and a low gate for children, in Buckinghamshire

1   2

3, 4

2

1 A conically roofed summer house in white painted timber, designed by Marcus Edwards for his garden in Acton

2 An aviary in a grove of daturas and arum lilies in the garden of a villa in Tangier

3 An octagonal garden house in the Gothick taste in a London garden. Its architect was Philip Jebb ARIBA, and the echoing garden design is carried out in gravel, low box hedges, and paving setts by Peter Coats

4 A ball-capped gazebo with latticed window and white clapboard walls in the garden of The Ring, Audley End. In the foreground, an iron chair in the Gothick style

5 An airy pavilion, impractical as a shelter, but highly decorative, makes an attractive feature in the garden at Westend House, near Wickwar in Gloucestershire

1

2

1 A 'crystal bower' with glass walls and a transparent roof of plastic provides a warm, sunlit shelter even in winter. At Maenan Hall, Llanrwst, North Wales

2 A towering weeping willow gives the scale for this miniature garden pavilion of red brick

3 A greenhouse in romantic Gothick taste at Glenveagh Castle. Its design was based on a sketch by Philippe Jullian, and the architects were Patrick and Michael Scott

4 The Temple of Diana, of which the architect was James Paine (1716–1789), is as perfect an example of Georgian architecture as you could find anywhere

4

2

1 'Lattice-work can add distinction to the façade of any loggia,' such as this one recently made in the stables, of Avington Park in Hampshire

2 The summer house at Alderley Grange, Wotton-under-Edge in Gloucestershire. It is unusually sited in the angle of two garden walls and has a carved pediment and central supporting pillar. The seat is in the Chinese Chippendale style

3 A garden loggia carried out in the simplest materials, but totally successful owing to the fantasy and imagination of its design. In Edwin Smith's garden at Saffron Walden

4 A summer house with Gothick details, designed by Ben Porter for the garden at Kilmore in Bampton

WALLS, FENCES AND GATES

A garden, like a house, should have decorative walls and well-proportioned doorways

A walled garden is every gardener's dream: a garden completely surrounded with walls of brick or stone, to keep it snug and secret from unexpected visitors, whether rabbits or relations. A garden with brick walls furnished with peach trees, or stone walls curtained with roses, is surely the ideal.

The earliest walled gardens were created in Tudor times, and up till the eighteenth century, Miles Hadfield, the celebrated garden expert, tells us 'a garden without a wall would have been unthinkable except, possibly, in some districts where the water-table was high and a moat had, at an early stage, been dug to keep out marauders. William Lawson in his book *A New Orchard & Garden*, published in James I's reign, listed these as deer, goats, sheep, hares, rabbits, cattle and horses—all of which, until the days of enclosures, would be wandering about. (To these, of course, were added two-legged animals. It must be remembered that barbed wire and wire-netting, the panacea for all these evils, was a mid-nineteenth-century invention.) Even earlier than that, the word garden itself is usually said to be evolved from a word meaning an enclosed space. Our first gardens were certainly within monastery walls.'

Today, to enclose a garden of even a quarter of an acre would be an immense expense—especially if the traditional materials for garden walls, brick or stone, were chosen. But effective walls can be built in less expensive media. Breeze blocks, pierced brick, or prefabricated concrete in sections, are all possible materials and, if thoughtfully used, can be built into attractive walling.

When building a wall two necessities must always be remembered.

1 Fortunate is the garden planner who has some old ruins in which to make his garden. Today the ancient walls of the old Banqueting Hall of Halnaker House in Sussex are hung with tapestries of roses
2 Delicate iron gates at Cliveden in Buckinghamshire

2

1

2

1 An open-work wall of bricks to break, but not entirely exclude, the wind. There are still such walls in existence which are several hundred years old

2 A circular moon-gate in Essex, surmounted by white stone finials, at Hill Pasture near Dunmow

3 Vertically hanging cushions of aubretia growing in the crevices of a grey stone wall in the Cotswolds

4 Light-leaved Hydrangea integerrima is an excellent wall shrub as it is self-clinging, and decorates, without smothering, a wall

5 A low wall of sun-faded brick divides the terrace at Fingringhoe Hall in Essex from the rest of the garden.

6 An imaginatively designed gate can give character to the simplest garden scene

7 'Actinidia Kolomikta is a shrub with climbing tendencies . . . it is a very special plant, with its leaves splashed with white and crimson'

8 Architectural plants, such as acanthus and Yucca filamentosa, and a wall decorated with 'cockle shells all in a row', in an Islington garden

The first is that the foundations must be well prepared. The second is more often overlooked: this is the importance of a coping which will protect the structure of the wall from water seeping into it and freezing, which can result in cracking the wall from top to bottom. Brick walls are often given copings of stone—of more bricks—and in some gardens in the west of England, of thatch. Such copings not only protect the structure of the wall, but also shelter the fruit trees or climbers which have been planted against it.

In large gardens in the seventeenth and eighteenth centuries walls were constructed with built-in flues—through which warm air from stoves was conducted to heat the wall, encourage the ripening of fruit, and protect it from frost. But the well-informed Miles Hadfield tells us: 'In 1845 the tax was taken off glass. The price fell from 1s. 2d. to 2d. a foot. It was now cheaper to provide a glazed frame against a wall than to provide any heating.'

The Planting of Walls

No garden wall, even if it is of the most perfect Elizabethan brick, should stand naked to the eye. But there are the right and wrong plants with which to clothe walls. Ivy, wistaria, roses, clematis are all too familiar to need more than a passing note—though ivy should be used with the greatest circumspection, for its roots and tentacles can be destructive. But there are many plants which are perfect wall shrubs, some quite tender, which not only enhance the beauty of the wall they dress, but also because the added protection enables them to flourish as they would never do in the open. It is as simple as that. All the shrubs we

loosely class as wall-shrubs would grow perfectly happily free-standing in year-round mild climates, but due to the rigours of winter and early spring in northern regions, they benefit immensely from the protection of a wall.

Mention should also be made of some shrubs it is wrong to suppose must always be grown against a wall. For instance the handsome Buddleia alternifolia is quite tough enough to be grown in the open and looks far better than cramped against a wall, and only allowed one-sided living room. And it might be pointful, in passing, to name one shrub at least—Euonymus radicans variegata—which is usually grown for ground cover, but has only to be planted against a wall to exhibit marked climbing qualities, and to look most effective, too.

How far from the wall should you plant wall shrubs? In France, a belief persists that one metre is the minimum distance. Perhaps this is so for fruit trees, for which maximum moisture is necessary, but for the general run of wall-shrubs it is excessive. The soil at the base of walls is certainly apt to be dry—but the roots of a healthy well-planted shrub, especially if given some peat to retain moisture and well-rotted manure when set, should quickly spread away from the stock to find the damper soil nearby. Roots should never be too pampered, and a wide-spreading root system helps the development of full and luxuriant top growth. In more northern climes decorative shrubs are not expected to bear juicy fruit but only to look attractive and healthy; 18 inches is considered quite far enough from the base of the wall for planting. Of course, the lime to be found in the foundations of some walls must be taken into consideration. But that is a different problem. No gardener could expect a calcifuge, like a camellia, to flourish on a diet of mortar rubble, though other plants, such as buddleias and romneyas, would enjoy it.

What, then, are the best wall-shrubs to choose? Mention has already been made of the ceanothus, for these are wall shrubs *par excellence*, and the best of the early-flowering varieties are floribundus, thyrsiflorus and veitchianus. These all flower in early summer. Autumnal Blue, on the other hand, flowers from July onwards, as does burkwoodii. Spring-flowering ceanothus should be pruned back after they have flowered, and the later flowerers in the early spring. If planted against a wall, most ceanothus can attain twenty feet or more.

Another plant which few gardeners would think of growing in the open, though it would doubtless survive—just—is Choisya ternata, a white-flowered shrub that comes out in early spring, with strongly aromatic leaves, named after the famous eighteenth-century Swiss botanist, M. J. D. Choisy.

The chaenomeles are usually grown against a wall. The new hybrid quinces offer a range of colours unknown fifty years ago, and their flowers are particularly welcome as they are among the earliest of spring. Knaphill Scarlet lives up to its name, while nivalis is white. All

4

1 Clematis montana is familiar to everyone, and gives a galaxy of starry flowers every May. C.m. rubens is a pink variety which is less vigorous
2 A white garden door is given character by an elegant motif in metal, and a lavish planting on either side of Cotoneaster horizontalis
3 Wistaria sinensis is another climber which enhances, without overwhelming, a wall
4 Lewisia with striped chintzy flowers of pink and white, growing in a trellis-topped wall in the garden at Bodnant in North Wales

1 Black-painted iron gates high-lighted in gold, in a Scottish garden
2 A gate of such spidery elegance as to seem unreal, invites the visitor to sylvan solitude

chaenomeles flower over a long period, for which reason they are called by the Chinese 'the flower of a hundred days'.

A shrub which looks as if nature designed it to grow on walls, so affectionately does it hug them, is Cotoneaster horizontalis, often growing seven or eight feet up a wall with no artificial aid. It can be seen in the picture shown on page 122. Like all the cotoneasters, it is completely tolerant as to soil. Its white flowers in spring are beloved of bees and its berries in autumn make it a gay sight as days grow shorter. Its cousin, Cotoneaster salicifolia, also makes an effective wall-shrub with its elegant growth, delicate willow-like leaves and scarlet berries.

Several of the excellent family of viburnum are best grown on walls—especially V. burkwoodii which has fragrant flowers in clusters five inches across. These show up brilliantly against the background of a wall. Another viburnum, V. rhytidophyllum—a splendid evergreen with leaves like ancient book-leather, heavily felted underneath—thrives in the protection of a wall. Reginald Farrer—the well-known plant collector, who wrote so well about plants, and whose *English Rock Garden* is a classic—described V. rhytidophyllum as 'the pew-opener', so dignified an appearance does a well-grown plant present.

The deciduous Actinidia Kolomikta is a shrub with climbing tendencies which should always be planted in the shelter of a wall. It is a very special plant, with its leaves splashed with white and crimson, a curiosity of colouring which becomes more marked as the season advances.

Pyracanthas, though perfectly hardy in the open, are much used as wall-shrubs where their berries enliven the autumn scene. P. angustifolia often holds its crimson fruit all winter through, and P. rogersiana flava has berries of a clear and pleasing yellow.

Piptanthus nepalensis is one of the leguminosae and a relative of the laburnum (it is also sometimes known as Piptanthus laburnifolius). The two plants bear a definite resemblance, though piptanthus is infinitely more distinguished looking with its larger, nearly evergreen leaves and gold rabbity pea-flowers. It prefers wall protection and well-drained soil.

Hydrangea integerrima is another distinguished and little-grown wall shrub, which clings to its support with aerial roots. Its light-coloured evergreen leaves are its chief beauty.

Last in this list of wall shrubs is one which clothes many a Georgian façade with its aristocratic leaves, and has scented many a stately garden when its flowers open in late summer—magnolia. M. grandiflora is by far the best to plant for a wall and, if you can get it, the Exmouth variety. Like all the evergreen magnolias, it does not need to be in flower to be decorative, for its leaves of burnished green on top and velvety brown beneath, look attractive all the year round, while its enormous chalice-like flowers are exquisitely scented. Magnolia . . .

, 2 9

, 4 10

1 A classical white picket fence for a small house in Buckinghamshire

2 A fence of white-painted wood in a Chinoiserie design adds a note of sophistication to a field of daffodils in a Hampshire garden

3 A simple but attractive rustic weathered-wood fence on the Belvoir Castle estate. The lower, close-set bars keep out rabbits; the criss-cross upper part is light-looking and un-usual

4 Another version of the lattice fence. Carefully spaced uprights and cross-bars give it an almost Oriental feeling

5 Open-work lattice fencing which enables the free circulation of air

6 An almost too elaborate fence, too low to be of practical use. Careful design of fences such as these is very important.

7 Under a neat fence of planking are cushions of the low-growing aromatic-leaved Santolina chamae-cyparissus

8 A neat and practical version of a Chinese Chippendale fence which would keep any garden secure from straying dogs

9 This unusual balustrade with its Sun-in-Splendour motif is at Schwetzingen, near Mannheim, where there is a garden laid out, about 1753, in the grandest way by the architect Nicholas Pigage for the Elector Carl Theodor

10 A low gate in the rococo style in the garden at Great Witley in Worcestershire

, 6

what a debt gardens all over the world owe to Pierre Magnol (1638–1715), if indeed it was he who introduced the magnolia to domestic horticulture, as well as providing it with such a mellifluous name. He might, after all, have been called Schmidt.

Pierre Magnol was born fifteen years after one of the greatest of all gardeners André Le Nôtre, creator of Vaux-le-Vicomte and Versailles, and gardener to Louis XIV. Well informed about most things, the great Le Nôtre knew little about wall-shrubs, and though one cannot imagine even the most beautiful magnolia looking anything but absurd on the walls of Versailles, he decreed—and his dicta were, in his time, decrees—that there should be a surface completely bare of plants equal to the width of any building's shadow. And he was wrong in the opinion that planting too close to an outside wall attracts damp. The reverse is true; most shrubs take in water by the roots, which helps to keep the area

, 8

1 A garden wall in Gloucestershire is given grandeur by the addition of an imposing arch of dressed stone
2 Trim urn-shaped finials give point and dignity to a white wood gate at Great Hundredge Manor in Buckinghamshire
3 Two smiling Putti from the Brenta in Italy, surmount sturdy pillars flanking a garden gate at Tyninghame in Scotland
4 An unusually light looking gate in cast iron between two terraces in an Essex garden
5 A white iron gate in a rose hung wall in Wiltshire
6 Star-capped double gates under a vine-covered arch in the garden of architect Clough Williams Ellis at Plas Brondanw, Merioneth, in Wales
7 The 'Fish Gate' at Kinross House on the shores of Loch Leven
8 A wooden door with a thistle window in the garden at Earlshall in Fife
9 A white gate with close-set dog-bars in an arch of yew, at Daneway House, in the Cotswolds
10 Wrought iron fencing and gate with boldly architectural piers topped with eagles in Coade stone, at Launceston in Cornwall

round the house dry. But before planting an Exmouth Magnolia, a Ceanothus burkwoodii or Actinidia Kolomikta, the purity and fertility of the soil should be checked—especially if there has been any recent new construction. All sorts of toxic materials, such as paint, may have destroyed the natural goodness in the ground; so fresh soil may have to be imported.

The width of the flower bed around the house depends of course upon the size of the latter; the higher the house, the bigger the bed.

Fences

Ideally, of course, gates and fences should have no place in a garden. They suggest confinement, whereas almost all modern gardeners have been at pains to suggest that the primary requirement in garden design is to imply a sense of freedom. We are to think of our gardens as if they were untrammelled by boundaries, continuing onwards and outwards as a kind of limitless Elysium. 2, 3,

But realities are different. Other people have gardens. Definition is required. In 1618, William Lawson devoted a complete chapter to fencing, and, as already mentioned, listed the animal enemies of the gardener.

Nowadays our garden enemies are probably fewer. Our need is basically to make clear to our neighbours the limits of our own boundaries so that the deeds to our property, which are doubtless locked in a bureau drawer, are matched by an outdoor statement of our possessions. All very selfish, no doubt, but a necessary evil in a predatory, land-hungry world.

Lawson was in favour of a fairly formidable kind of fencing. Thorn hedges allied with ditches and moats he deemed the most satisfactory. Most of us would now settle for something less substantial.

Fences, and walls, for that matter, looked intimidating in the seventeenth century; 'climb over if you dare' would seem to have been the legend which should, most honestly, have been carved upon their iron-work or stout timbers. The function of walls and fences was plainly to exclude rather than to welcome. They thus became unclimbably high and difficult to look over. And if trespass was possible, which it seldom was, trespassers were duly prosecuted. Walls were the most stalwart of all protective boundaries, of course; there is the sad story of Vanbrugh being forced to see something of his handiwork at Blenheim, after his row with the Duchess, by peering over the wall. 5, 6,

Over the centuries, the more forbidding aspects of fencing have changed. Today a boundary fence just marks a boundary—nothing more. Its construction may successfully keep out dogs, but seldom offers a serious hazard to a man. What was once a form of defence has become a decorative device. Gone are the days of the great iron-smiths with Jean Tijou at their head; though much of their finest work from the 8, 9, 1

1

2   3

seventeenth and eighteenth centuries is still standing. But it is still possible to have very handsome fences to suit the most extrovert personalities. But most of us will settle for less. Fortunately, whether of ironwork, picket wood, clapboard, wattle or overlap, there is sufficiency of fences to offer the property-owner endless opportunities for adding a pleasing feature to the immediate setting of his house.

There are so many different ways of treating fences. Ironwork—preferably wrought and not cast, which is inclined to have a cumbersome look—need not always be black. It can be painted white, especially if against a dark background of evergreens, or even touched discreetly with gold, or painted like the railings that once were at Versailles, and still are at the Grand Trianon—a triumphant blue. Wooden fences can be had in many different designs, and of course a white picket fence can be pretty in a dozen different ways. But whatever colour or design you devise for your fences remember to make them smiling and welcoming. Their message should be 'Come in', rather than 'Keep out'.

Timber

Wood, as we have noted, is the most suitable material for fencing—though in this utilitarian age concrete, wattle and, of course, iron and wire are often employed. But wood is what we think of when we plan a fence. It is odd, because by all the laws of logic, timber should no longer be used in half the spheres in which it still serenely and congenially continues to hold an unchallenged place. In shipbuilding, for instance, we still see timber used as widely in the building of great ships as in the making of dinghies, despite the employment of a hundred new materials in liners and an increasing use of fibreglass for small boats.

So, too, in the garden.

Despite its claims to far greater durability, ironwork has never yet ousted timber from its manifold decorative uses in the garden. Despite its increasing use in the construction of greenhouses, aluminium has not yet replaced timber in the kitchen garden.

The ease of handling and working timber is, of course, one reason for its popularity, allied with the rise of the do-it-yourself habit. For every handyman who prefers to work with forge and solder, a hundred would rather work with plane and saw.

The overwhelming advantage of wood for garden furniture and other decorative features lies in its innate naturalness. There is a fitness for purpose and subtle sense of rightness in the use of timber in the garden, the sheer, appealing, sympathetic nature of wood, unadorned or painted.

Painting is an important factor in the use of wood. We appreciated the sombre majesty of the dark rafters of Westminster Hall, seen at their

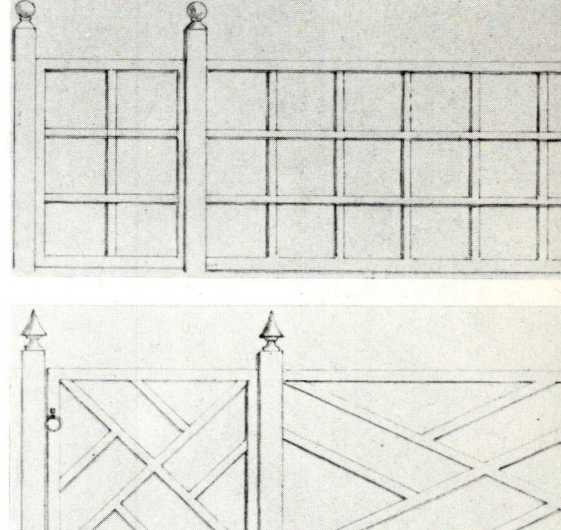

4

1 A design for a garden behind a house on East 38th Street, New York, devised by Peter Coats, and drawn by Hugh Robson
2 An attractive example of a white wooden picket gate in a garden in Worcestershire. The contrast between the spacing of the upper bars and the lower dog-bars is particularly happy
3 Trellis in the grand manner, with a trompe l'oeil invitation to further romantic vistas, drawn by Hugh Robson. This sort of elaborate treillage was first used in the formal gardens of eighteenth-century France, but it is still effective for 'enlarging' town gardens and not too difficult to achieve
4 Designs for decorative fencing by Hugh Robson

1

most inspiring during the lying-in-state of Sir Winston Churchill, and
we can recognize that the Accademia Bridge in Venice needs a darken-
ing preservative, but in our gardens, woodwork should almost always
be as gleaming white as paint and care can make it.

Gates

We admire handsome wrought iron gates when we see them set at the
entrances to great houses, held between tall piers, surmounted by lead
eagles or deer or stone urns or pineapples.

But when it comes to gates for our own more modest domains we
turn instinctively to timber. And thanks to the inventiveness of Chippendale and the earlier masters of Chinoiserie and Gothick, we have a
vast number of prototypes from which to choose.

2

Gates, besides being decorative and inviting, must also be practical. If of wooden, or iron bars they must be provided with dog-bars at their base to keep out unwanted four-footed friends. They must shut securely, and be sturdily hung between strong piers.

Gates in the well-furnished garden can add immeasurably to the garden's character. How often, in our childhood, has a locked garden gate disappointed us? And to find a garden gate unexpectedly unlocked is as much a thrill for grown-ups as for children. Miles Hadfield explained it well when he wrote: 'I am surprised that garden gates have not been the subject of study by psychologists as examples of something comparable to the fashionable love-hate relationship: a longing to pass beyond them and see what they only partially conceal—most seem singularly designed and placed to arouse this emotion—balanced against

1 Square trellis is preferable to trellis work in a diamond pattern, as is seen in this neatly paved, closely planted Chelsea garden
2 A roof garden in London has trellised walls and, for a centre piece, a giant basket-formed flower bed in white iron work

1 A statue in white marble is given a setting of trellis in trompe l'oeil
2 Treillage in the grandest manner, where the woodwork, laid square on square, one layer straight, one layer diagonal, conjures an elaborate design

a prohibition to do so. The excitement of unexpectedly breaking through this barrier into a garden—which many of us have on occasion been guilty of doing—heightened in the mind of a child, is nowhere more truly described than in Frances Hodgson Burnett's *The Secret Garden*.'

And one might add *Alice in Wonderland*, too: as her sigh comes down over the years to us. . . 'How shall I ever get into that beautiful garden?'

Trellis

A touch of *treillage* brings practical and airy elegance to the garden, though it's a far cry from the vine 'engrapid' Tudor arbours of rough trellis-work to the super sophisticated trellis-work pavilions of Versailles, and a further cry from there to the treillage which makes such a practical, and pretty screen in so many city gardens. And yet some of the most romantic settings man has ever devised have been built in trellis-work. The fascinating, ever-changing patterns of light and shadow it creates can turn even a backyard into a place of romantic enchantment. Today the great qualities of this centuries-old form of decorative construction are being recognized again as a building material for both exteriors and interiors, but especially in the garden.

Traditional treillage consists of nothing more than thin slats of wood criss-crossed and nailed to a frame. But the strips can be crossed and re-crossed in countless ways to produce an almost infinite variety of patterns; even a change of scale creates an entirely different look. Cleverly designed trellis-work can create space, and the false perspectives conjured will make small gardens look larger. Furthermore, out-of-door woodwork can now be weatherproofed with painted-on preservatives, or it can be constructed of a tough weather-resistant redwood, which looks handsome and needs no painting.

The uses of treillage are almost as numerous as its patterns, even without the use of false perspective. A treillage enclosure can make any space—a patio, a garden, a terrace—seem larger than if left open, yet it achieves this magic without cutting off light or air. And as a background for plants, treillage works hand in glove with nature, providing support and protection, unaccompanied by excessive shade. In eighteenth-century France, where lattice-work reached its peak of splendour, it was used to make extravagant pavilions and lavish arbours. Currently the subject of a popular revival it has been widely used out-doors in a more modest manner—for garden gates, summer-houses, gazebos, or, even more matter-of-factly, to screen a back-door area, or garage.

Treillage can smarten up the dullest garden. It can be painted a crisp white, crow-black, or the wood can be left its natural colour. In France trellis is often painted green—not the dead green of a Victorian garden fence, but the green of vine leaves, sprayed with sulphate of ammonia, which enhances but does not compete with the green of living leaves.

WATER IN THE GARDEN

provides the treasures and the pleasures of reflection and recreation

Although gardeners and gardening writers may disagree, sometimes even violently, upon such matters as the questionable splendours of herbaceous borders; the organic or inorganic approach to soil rejuvenation; the desirability of cultivating a blue rose, they all seem agreed that the gardener, who, by providence or a strong right arm, is possessed of water in one form or another on his estate, whether miniscule back garden or majestic broad acres, is particularly blessed.

> 'Water is living . . . springs from earth,
> Whether from mountains poured in melting stream
> Or risen in the stones, a bubbling birth
> Struck by some Moses from a sombre dream . . .'

So wrote Victoria Sackville-West, novelist, poet and gardener-extraordinary in her poem *The Garden*, and although the language is high-flown, its general tenor can readily be appreciated and approved by most of us.

But not every tyro gardener is immediately aware of the treasure and pleasure he has at his command in the possession of water, although not all are as honest as the Victorian Poet Laureate, Alfred Austin, in his endearing confession: 'I abolished a pond near the north gate leading into the lane . . . regarding it as shockingly unsightly, and replacing it with a mixed copse. How often have I wished that pond back again, that I might grow water-lilies on its surface, irises on its bank, and reeds and aquatic plants all about it.' Better perhaps to have water that one cannot exploit than no water at all, although that situation can have its galling

1 The Chinoiserie bridge at Mereworth Castle is a recent addition to the garden. Its design was taken from an old Dutch book on garden decoration, *Magazin van Tuinsieraden*

2 Lancelot 'Capability' Brown (1716–83) created the lake at Blenheim by damming the river Glyme. The park is considered to be one of the most beautiful in England

1

2

moments: so many people say, 'What splendid opportunities you must have for water-lilies and aquatic plants with the New River running through the garden.' So many, in fact, wrote E. A. Bowles in *My Garden in Summer*, 'that some day I shall push one of them into it instead of explaining that, if I did plant a Water Lily in the River, the Water Board's officials would soon rake it out again, and, even if they did not, it would catch its death of cold.'

Having decided that almost any kind of water is better than none, we quickly realize that there are here, as in most other gardening delights, classifications of pleasure.

Water with a hard, naked edge and little or no vegetation is scarcely ever good to look at. A margin of rich, living plants is better for fish and game as well as for effect. A transformation is required. Fortunately the waterside plants one may establish are worth having by any standards.

But perhaps the most beautiful of all water gardens are river and stream gardens. Francis Bacon summed it up neatly—as he usually did—in his essays *Of Gardens*. 'The main point', he wrote, 'is that the water be in perpetual motion, fed by a water higher than the pool, and delivered into it by fair spouts and then discharged away again underground.' The form of such *mouvementé* water is usually far more interesting, visually, than anything we can make ourselves, and the vegetation is often good without overmuch care. Yet, with a little thought, we can make such waters even more interesting. Bacon, however, was pessimistic about pools which, he contended, make the garden 'unwholesome and full of flies and frogs.' No lily ponds for him.

1 Water is seldom as effective as when it is cleaved by swimming swans, as it is in the baroque garden of Veitshöchheim near Würzburg in Bavaria
2 This building, with its oriental roof-line and elegant verandah, was built in the eighteenth century as a fishing pavilion. Extended later, it now makes an enviable waterside retreat. The Quarters House, near Wivenhoe in Essex
3 One massive stone slab makes a sturdy bridge in a corner of the garden at Burford House in Worcestershire
4 Two giant stones make a Japanese-inspired bridge over a stream in the water garden at Cliveden. To the right, and in matching scale, the huge leaves of Gunnera manicata

Fountains

Ever since the earliest times, the fountain has been man's friend. The word *fontana* in Italian derives from the Latin *fons*—a beginning or source—hence 'fountain head', and the French word for a fountain or spring is *source*.

Whether falling into a pool or stone receptacle, offering water for drinking or cultivation, or, as a springing jet (for fountains always either fall or rise—sometimes both) the fountain has always played the beneficent role of affording refreshment to the body or refreshment to the eye.

It could be said that there is a place in any garden, large or small, for a fountain. Versailles has its Grandes Eaux, visited by thousands every Sunday. The water toys at the Villa d'Este inspired Liszt to compose his most moving music. And in that same marvellous garden there is, or was, a water organ which impressed Montaigne, though it disappointed the more captious John Evelyn . . . because it only played one tune. In Washington there is the celebrated fountain which tosses its jet hundreds of feet in the air in salute to the Lincoln Memorial.

In our own gardens—our half-acre Villa d'Estes and pocket-handkerchief Versailles—more modest fountains could find a place, and water could make the music of our gardens as it did for the Moors in the Alhambra.

Any medium-sized garden could find space for one slim and soaring jet, and in the smallest plot a place could be found for water falling in quiet, but not noiseless, drops into a stone or marble basin. The half-heard sound of water on a hot day is the most soothing sound in the world.

But only if your fountain basin is of a certain size should you introduce goldfish: these do not like water which is perpetually disturbed. One has always felt concerned for Tennyson's 'Gold fin in the porphyry font', being continually buffeted about by the fountain's fall, and, you may be certain, without any weeds or green for privacy or shelter. No fountain greenery for that poor fish.

Neither should you grow water-lilies too near a fountain's spray; the water will spoil the purity of their petals. All water-surface plants prefer to grow in water that is still.

Water and Waterside Plants

The water-margin offers to lovers of hardy flowers a site easily made into a handsome garden. Too often aquatic plants only are used in such places, and of these usually a very meagre selection; while the improvement of the waterside may be most readily effected by planting the banks near with vigorous hardy flowers, as many of the finest plants, from irises to globe flowers, thrive in moist soil. Bank plants have this advantage over water plants, that we can fix their position, whereas water plants—especially water-lilies, spread so much that some kinds over-run others. There is an example of this on page 143.

In order to be effective, the outline of any man-made pool, pond or lake ought not only to be irregular, but it ought also to be in accordance with the laws of nature. As, in most cases, the natural pond or lake is merely an expanded stream or river, we can look to the bank-lines of the latter for guidance in the forming of artificial ponds.

As a basis from which to start, a fairly sound axiom is that if it is to look as natural as possible your pool should have its largest and boldest recesses opposite, or nearly opposite, the largest promontory on the other side; and the bank-line should not terminate abruptly, but should form a slope continued below the water level.

In planting the shore of a pond or lake, it is the ground which projects into the water which should be furnished with the largest and boldest plants. This is not only perfectly natural, but has also the effect of partially concealing some of the recesses of the water. A pond, thus treated, will appear larger than it really is, and the walk around the bank will reveal fresh surprises with every step.

2

3

1 Water falls on water. The dolphin fountain in the centre of the lily-strewn lake at Powerscourt Castle in Ireland
2 The Eagle Fountain at the Villa d'Este at Tivoli, near Rome, one of the most famous water gardens in the world, and much admired by John Evelyn on his visit three hundred years ago
3 Water falls from a lion's mask into an upturned flower-shaped bowl, over a circular goldfish pond in a garden in Chelsea.

The water-soaked margins of ponds and brooks can provide a home for many graceful fine-foliaged and flowering plants. One of the noblest of our plants with large leaves, delighting in such a position, is Gunnera manicata, a giant Brazilian native which, with some care, will condescend to thrive in the north. Other effective plants which delight in riparian life, which, in fact, will hardly survive without permanently wet feet, are Butomus umbellatus, the flowering rush, the Bog Arum and the golden Marsh Marigold, Calla palustris, Iris japonica (one of the few iris which will grow in damp), Mimulus luteus, the Water Musk and the arrow-shaped and named sagittaria. Most important water plants of all—the nymphaeas, or Water Lilies—deserve a few paragraphs of their own.

A pool for water-lilies, or water-lilies grown on a lake, are a garden tradition as old as rose-gardens, though the colourful and hardy water-lilies we know today were only introduced in the last hundred years, many by the great French gardener, Latour-Marliac. These new and spectacular hybrids were at once acclaimed by gardeners, who soon discovered, furthermore, that these beautiful flowers could be grown, not only on large lakes, but in ponds a few feet across, in the smallest gardens.

2

Water-lilies are not difficult to grow, for once they are established they look after themselves. Weather hardly affects them, and they are prone to few diseases. They do not ask for fertilizer or tying-up, or cossetting. In the hottest, dryest weather they look cool and fresh. In short they are almost fool-proof.

From April till the first frosts their foliage—often beautifully marbled —looks handsome, and they flower for months. Few plants give so much for so little attention.

Water-lilies grow in ordinary, good soil which, in a constructed pool, should be at least six inches deep. They like full sun, although they will grow in shade, but will then produce flowers much less freely. The water may vary in depth, according to the varieties grown, from a few inches to a couple of feet.

A few of the best varieties of water-lilies, in colours, are the white Gladstoniana and odorata alba, the rose-coloured marliaca carnea (called after the master hybridist) and Mrs. Richmond, the crimson Escarboucle and James Brydon, and the yellow Sunrise.

Like most healthy plants, if given conditions they like, water-lilies will spread rapidly; though their flowers, in a mass, are poignantly beautiful, they lose their charm when they spread over the whole of the

1 A garden half-carpeted with water —square flagstones lead between slender flag leaves, floating lilies and spidery Butomus umbellatus in a garden near Paris
2 Water lilies may soon obscure the water of this circular pool, in the garden at Tintinhull in Somerset

1 A screen of open work concrete filters the breezes blowing from the Beaulieu River. A free-form swimming-pool in Hampshire
2 High glass doors lead from the living-room of this house in Washington to the terrace pool, walled for shelter and for privacy

sheet of water so that even waterfowl cannot make their way through them. To be unable to see a pool for the water-lilies is even worse than obliterating the wood with the trees. So when planting, leave a good space between the clumps: and do not forget the necessity for a good garden seat at the water-side. Here is one place where the cares of the frenetic world can be exorcised. It is surprising how many people will make a pool, plant it, and then forget this essential complement to water's soothing balms.

Pools for Pleasure

Until comparatively recently a swimming pool was (1) a status symbol; (2) rectangular; (3) a bother in the winter months because (a) it was out of use and (b) it looked cold and uninviting, especially if covered with a quilted floating cover to keep it free of leaves.

Not one of these itemized limitations now need apply. As a status symbol the pool now ranks well below a hard tennis-court or a coloured television set. As a shape, the pool of today knows no boundaries, or at least acknowledges only those imposed by the buyer. As for its winter drawbacks, the pool can now prove as pleasurable an amenity as in the best of summer months. New water-heating methods and better-designed mobile covers have made the pool a year-round institution.

Army or marine engineers can always be counted on to have their own pet structures for capturing solar heat—but the average householder usually has a greater belief in the figures of the heating engineers.

In a Northern summer you will obviously need some form of heating, either by gas, electricity or oil. You will usually need a boiler which is separate from the house heating system: the heater can easily be placed alongside the filter plant and the whole concealed in an outhouse or behind a screen. In choosing the size of heater, remember that installation will probably cost about 15 per cent of the total price of the pool. Running costs will relate, naturally, to the size of the pool and the price of the particular fuel, but you should estimate about 0·4 therms per day per 1000 gallons of pool water.

If these figures seem rather high, there are, of course, ways of conserving heat. Covering the pool day and night when not in use is one way. Most manufacturers will supply covers; or you can make your own. On a small pool you can use polythene sheeting attached to wooden frames, but perhaps more effective are polystyrene blocks which float on the water and can reduce heat-loss by nearly half. Shrubs or screens on the windward side of an open pool will also help.

Cost is, of course, the operative factor governing the building of any pool in any garden, but judging by the increasing number of pools on the outskirts of most large cities, which can be seen by any traveller arriving by air, a surprising number of householders are finding the installation costs within their budgets—and in these days the domestic

2

1 The garden designer René Péchère devised this fountain in the form of a single jet rising from a carved stone, shell-shaped basin. All around are Kurume azaleas

2 A fountain consisting of a slender soaring spray throws its water thirty feet high in the garden at Holker Hall, Cark in Cartmel in Lancashire. The rhododendron is a century-old arboreum

pool is scarcely the ideal subject on which to base a request for an overdraft to your bank manager.

The cost of a swimming pool varies a good deal, and depends very much on circumstances. For instance, if you live on a hill and want a pool even higher up the hill, it is obviously going to introduce some serious considerations for the estimation clerk. Free-form pools, as a general rule, cost more than the conventional square ones. In fact shape is now proving the pool-building industry's most intriguing problem: the choice seeming to be fairly evenly divided between the free-form and the rectangular form, curved at one end to accommodate segmental steps into the shallow end, known as the 'Roman design'.

Pool surrounds are also receiving rather more attention now from both manufacturers and their clients. Composition paving-stones are supplied by all manufacturers, but the contribution that a really adequate surround to a pool can make to the garden-setting is still too often forgotten. And this point is well worth a good deal of consideration, for a pool can frequently prove little more than a gleaming gash in a garden setting, a charmless *nouveau riche* innovation. By the sympathetic placing of walling, fencing, plants in tubs, urns, seats and a pool-house, the setting can be made a feature to enhance, not only the life of the garden, but also its visual charm.

2

1 A miniature lake, studded with red water lilies (Escarboucle), and grown about with luxuriant groups of waterside plants such as hosta, bergenia and lysimachia, at Bampton Manor in Oxfordshire

2 A ready-made lily pond of black glassfibre, with a surrounding rim for waterside plants. It can be placed in position, planted and filled in an afternoon

3 A piece of water, handsomely proportioned in the classic style, in the great American garden at Filoli, San Mateo, California

3

5

6

3

1 Water, paving stones and sharply contrasting foliage make a strongly textured picture when photographed from an upper window of this house in Holland Park. The garden was designed by artist Cyril Fradan

2 Square paving stones contain a bed for Japanese iris and other moisture-loving plants, in a garden in which water plays an important part

3 In the garden of a cottage at Laycock in Wiltshire, an irregularly shaped pond overhung with cushions of pinks

4 A wall fountain in blue and white faience in a garden in Chelsea

5 The smallest town garden can be given character and coolness on hot days, by a pond and a falling spray

6 A sunk garden in Mayfair with a circular, reed-grown pool. The garden lies between Hill Street and South Audley Street, in the heart of London's West End

7 A fountain pool from which the water escapes through a lead mask; large-leaved rheums grow beyond

7

1 A natural stream is the greatest asset any garden can have. This one, between luxuriantly planted banks, is at Mount Usher in Ireland

2 Water in action. A gushing stream issues from a baroque Italian mask at the Mill House, Sutton Courtenay in Berkshire

3 A bridge in the classic Japanese style, lacquered a dark sealing wax red, in the wild garden at Russborough in Co. Wicklow

4 A delicately arched bridge in a Chinese Chippendale design spans a stream in the garden at Stanton Harcourt Manor in Oxfordshire

5 A bridge in a Chinoiserie design spans a stretch of water in the garden at La Grange at Mortefontaine. One of the first bridges in this style was built by Sir William Chambers (1726–96), architect of the pagoda at Kew

6 A bridge, however simple, gives an air of interest, and invites the visitor to walk further

7 A simply constructed, but stylish, rustic bridge in a garden in Berkshire

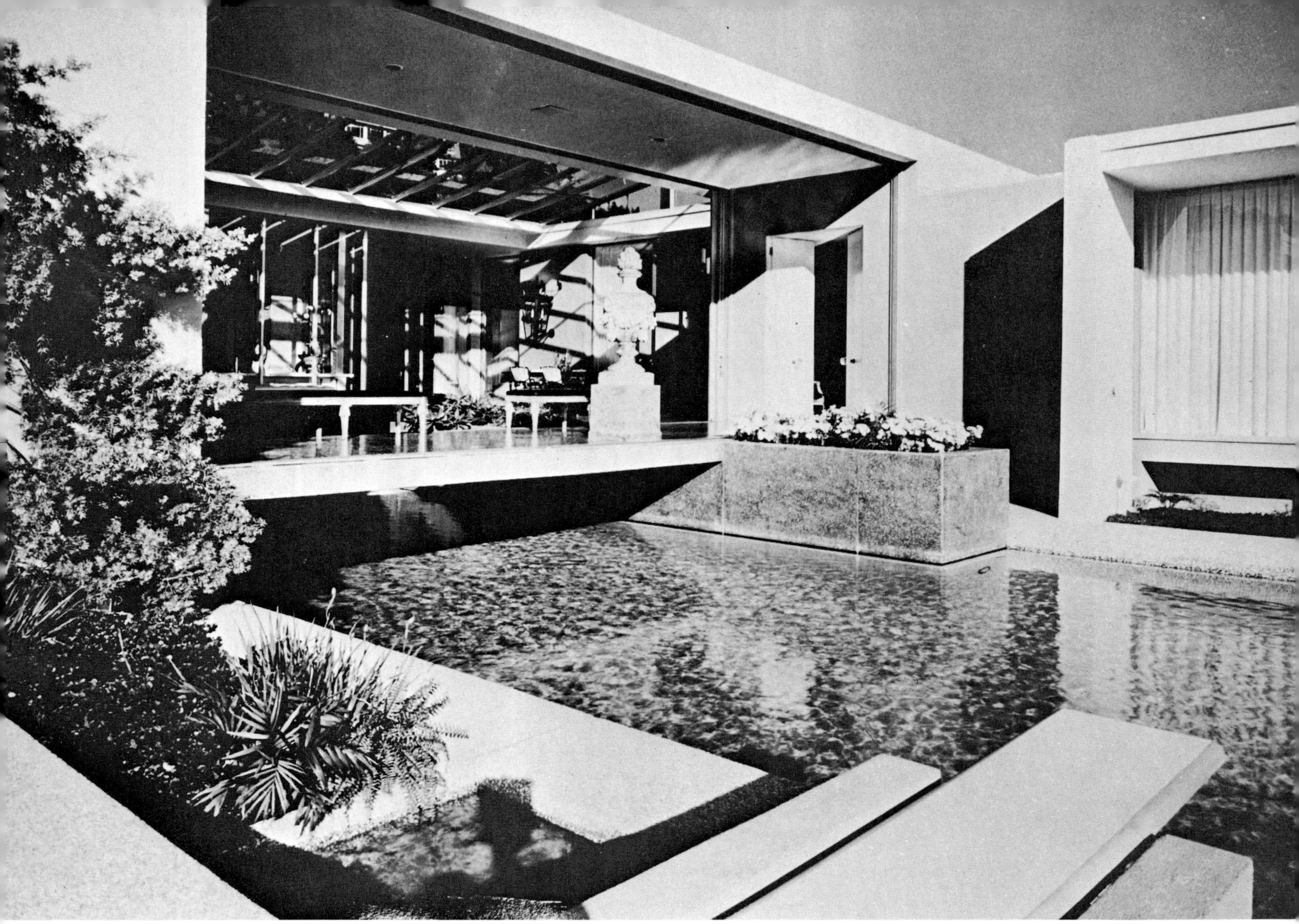

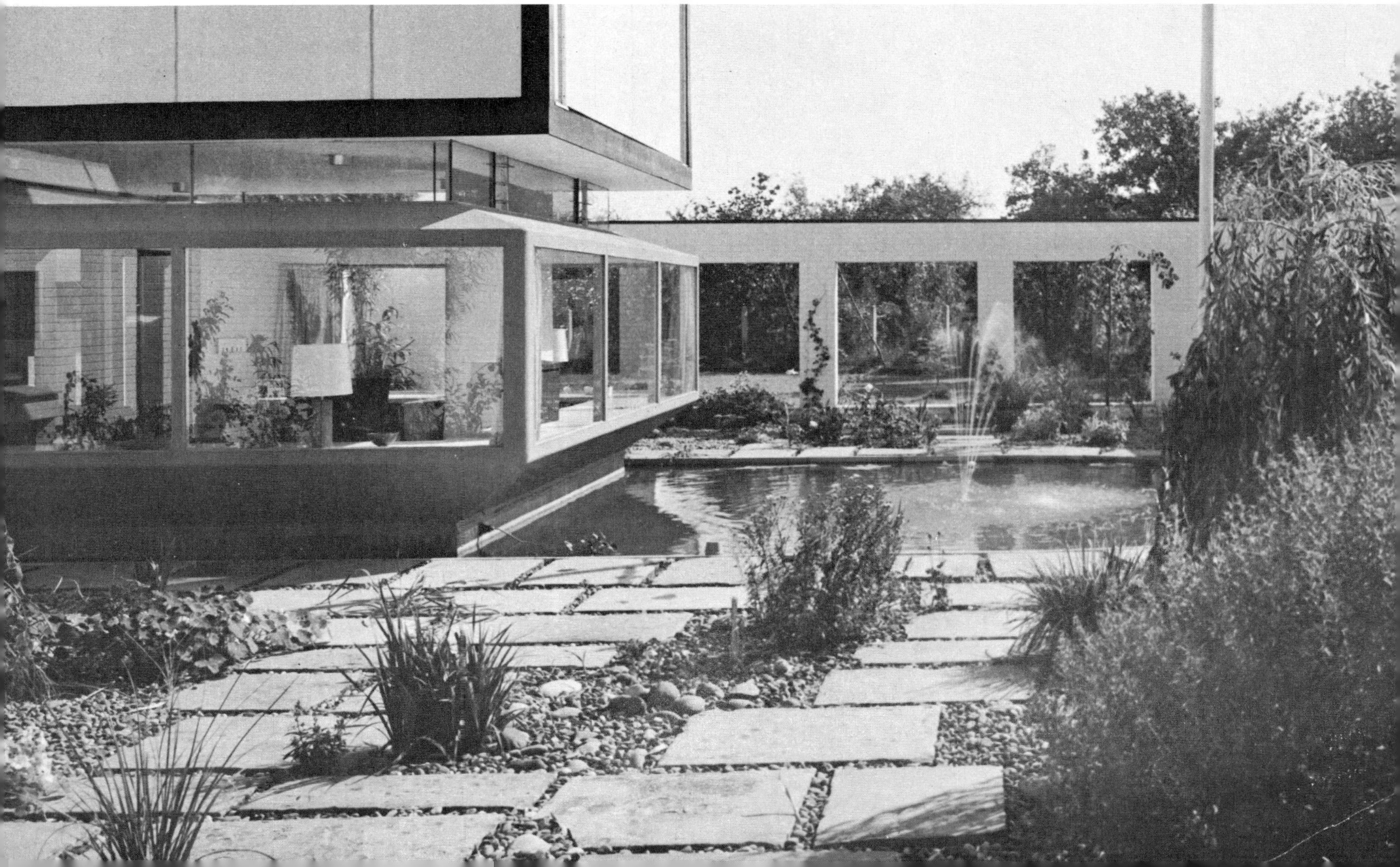

1 A swimming-pool half indoors, half outdoors, in Beverly Hills, California

2 An informally planted terrace surrounds, on three sides, this bow-shaped pool in a compound walled for privacy. Architect and owner, Keith Ingham

3 There can be few pools with as dramatic a view as this across the Mill Valley, California

4 Non-slip paving stones of concrete aggregate bridge this swimming-pool; these, with the overhanging wooden eaves, and understated greenery around, create an almost Japanese effect

1 In the famous garden at Dumbarton Oaks in Washington D.C. there is this subtly shaped pool half way down the Rock Creek Slope. Garden architect Beatrix Ferrand designed it in the 'twenties

2 The sunk garden in Kensington Gardens. Around the rectangular pool are tubs of flowers, and three seventeenth-century lead tanks are set in the water itself

3 A lily-strewn goldfish pond lies beneath the terrace of Boxted House on the Essex/Suffolk border

1

1 A black and white striped tent, with rust red roof, overlooks an outside swimming-pool in the Landes district of France. The ladder is movable

2 A poolside garden where the emphasis is on the 'architecture' supplied by the tailored trees and imposing plants. Between pots of pink geraniums is a sculpture by Signori, and the roof of the loggia is corniced with a hedge of ficus, grown in a copper-lined trough. The whole concept of this Palm Beach garden is daring, but totally successful

2

ART IN THE GARDEN

Art, artefact and artifice, all can play an important part in garden decoration

How large must your garden be before you can indulge in sculpture? Perhaps Alexander Pope (1688–1744) can give us a clue to the answer. In two reassuring lines he informs us:

> 'He gains all ends who so pleasingly confounds
> Surprises, varies and conceals the bounds.'

Sculpture, with what might be termed its built-in talent for surprising, halting, holding or redirecting the eye, can certainly aid us in this harmless and rewarding endeavour. And the answer is, of course, you can have sculpture in any size of garden; for most gardens, large or small, are somewhere that sculpture—*avant garde* or eighteenth century, controversial or Victorian—can find a place, without being unduly outdistanced or outfaced.

This is because almost any garden has a God-given talent for absorbing almost any object. In time, of course, substantial natural growth will overgrow and submerge any man-made object, even cities, as the forests of Cambodia and South America amply demonstrate. But even the most civilized of garden settings will soften the most assertive angularities of modern sculpture, and into its more reticent ambience the seemingly outrageous novelties of the latest sculpting genius will be absorbed. But this, of course, is only the negative side of the story. Many examples of modern sculpture seem almost uncannily well-adapted to take a place in a garden: a background of trees and lawns seems their natural habitat. It is easy to see why: they play out one of the great basic plays of art, ancient or modern, in that they act as foils for

1 A graceful figure in Victorian terra-cotta stands among the flowers of musk rose Penelope, in the garden at Pusey House near Faringdon in Berkshire
2 Kneeling woman by F. E. McWilliam, 1947. Mr Roland Penrose's collection

2

each other in texture, shape and colour—a fact long since recognized by the Japanese.

Gardeners throughout the centuries have been tempted by the challenge of setting static and permanent stone or metal against transient flowers and foliage, and in daring, have left us innumerable enchantments, proving again and again that any garden, however small, can advantageously receive some piece of sculpture or statuary. Across the South Atlantic the great modern garden designer, Burle Marx, has shown, in his tropical gardens in Brazil, this same feeling for the juxtaposition of stone shapes against the most luxuriant, rampant and colourful of plantings.

In our own domestic settings we can adopt and adapt some of these inspirations from other lands. A block of stone, however crudely carved and rugged, is unlikely to spoil any sweep of lawn. The angularities of ironwork will never over-awe a fine tree. Indeed, each may well gain something from the other.

Henry Moore is one of the contemporary sculptors greatly attracted by Nature; in fact, he works in the country outside London. 'I draw all

2

my energy from Nature,' he says, and he gives that energy back with his monumental statues that, like trees, need light and space to live. Mr. W. J. Keswick has been bold enough to place Henry Moore's great mystical figure—his King and Queen—against a background of moorland in Scotland, and by doing so, has achieved a juxtaposition of truly awful (in the eighteenth-century sense) majesty.

But this does not only apply to Moore's work. All sculptors of today seem to find their environment in the heart of trees and meadows. Statues dwell more happily notched into a corner of a garden, in the depths of woods, or defined against the gentle contour of a hill.

But few lovers of modern art would have the sheer nerve (or the sheer currency) to emulate Joseph Hirshhorn, whose garden in Connecticut is used as setting for what is, without doubt, one of the most remarkable collections of modern sculpture in private ownership. Here, within the confines of a formal terrace, a work by Barbara Hepworth partners a dancer by Marino Marini and a nude by Lipchitz reclines by a huge composition by Henry Moore. Some are shown in this section.

Although no one could be unimpressed by the aesthetic convictions,

1 Reclining nude by Emilio Greco, 1951, in a garden in St. John's Wood 2 Sphinxes were much used in garden decoration in the eighteenth century. This trio keeps watch under the cedars of Chiswick House, where the garden was laid out by the Earl of Burlington in 1725

163

1 A grotesque mask set among roses on a brick wall
2 'Ogni pensiero voi'—a giant mouth offers hospitality to 'any philosopher' visiting the surprising statuary at Bomarzo near Viterbo
3 An airy rose-grown temple in white painted wire, given importance by being floored with rough cobbles set in cement. At Sutton Park, Sutton on the Forest, near York

dedication and single-mindedness of such a collector as Mr. Hirshhorn, and more than a little envious of his courage in displaying a plentitude of such works in his garden, the taste of many will still incline to sculpture, most of it quite modest in size, which dates from the eighteenth century or is inspired by the great period.

Whatever period we favour, whether we yearn for a Chadwick or a Cheere to set at the end of our lawn or against a background of laurels in our back garden, we know the effect, of stone against leaf, that we are after.

From Pliny the Younger—whose descriptions of his manifold villa projects with their statuary and fountains makes his one of the most appealing and civilized of those voices which speak to us from the ancient world—to Mr. Keswick and Mr. Wurtzburger, sculpture has been as appealing to the Man of Taste as to the Man of Achievement. One garden house is basically like another, whether gothic, classic or modern. One pool is basically like another, whether rectangular or free-form. But with sculpture, the choice is unlimited. If the patron is rich enough he can commission the most pre-eminent sculptor to carve a score of statues; if he is egomaniacal enough he can crowd his garden with his own work; if he is dotty beyond the psychologist's reach he can even introduce monsters and giantesses to dwarf those of the Villa Orsini at Bomarzo, surely one of the most spectacular examples in the world of the use or misuse of garden sculpture.

Urns and Pots

Of all the decorative items which can be added to a garden to give a sense of distance, to emphasize the dark depths of rhododendrons in abundance, to give point to a charming vista, none is more rewarding than a classical vase, whether of stone, composition, terracotta, or cast-iron.

The great garden-makers of the eighteenth century realized this. In their nostalgic rehashing of the classical scenes—supposedly, but improbably, of ancient Greece and Rome—urns had an even more prominent part to play than statuary, obelisks or fountains. After all, urns were more readily available or, at least, the craftsmen for their making were. They certainly produced a wide range, from simple stone urns of a classical Wedgwood simplicity to the complexities of carved stone and finely cast bronze.

How did the idea of plant containers start? Miles Hadfield wonders 'whether it was Adam or Eve who first discovered that a plant could be dug up from the soil of Eden and would grow quite happily in some sort of container. Possibly it was Adam, with a view to earlier crops of apples. If so, then we may give the credit to Eve for the more surprising discovery that a flower, quite detached from the plant that bears it, will thrive, at least for a time, with its stem inserted in water.

2

1 Since the great days of garden embellishment, in the late seventeenth century, 'Caissons de Versailles' containing orange trees or clipped bays have been recognized garden ornaments
2 An informally planted terrace furnished with tubs of camellias, at the Round House, Netton, in Wiltshire

Pots and pans, ornamental in themselves and filled with growing plants, were certainly used skilfully by the Dutch in the sixteenth century. They can be seen in many Dutch paintings. In seventeenth-century pictures may be seen something very like the large, ornamented pots at Hever. In England, the title-page of Gerard's *Herball* showed some pleasantly-designed pots in 1597.

A century and a half later, with the coming of 'Capability' Brown, pots and pans full of plants were banished from gardens; they were replaced by very superior flowerless urns and vases, most carefully designed, and only placed after long deliberations over the rightness of their situations. Usually, they carried tasteful inscriptions, often to recall someone now deceased, possibly enshrining some abstract virtue, or drawing attention to the particular genius of the place.

Here one should remark on the subtle dictionary differences between an urn and a vase. The former is of roundish shape, which may be, but is not necessarily, used to contain the ashes of the dead. A vase is a taller, slenderer vessel, merely an ornament, or used on occasion for holding flowers.

Today a rich variety of urns and vases, and, indeed, quite common pots and pans, planted in styles that range from the traditional to the peculiar, are found in our gardens. They range from exquisite bronze urns such as those which decorated the garden at Bagatelle, by way of practical oil-jars like the one in the picture of Sissinghurst Castle (page 180), to simply shaped vases, of which the plants they contain are the feature. Some of the most beautiful of all are the basket-work pots that stand on the garden stairway at Powis Castle, which, ascending or descending, one sees first as striking silhouettes against the sky and then as rich patches of colour among the surrounding greenery (page 186).

And one should include the fashionable trough garden, though for my own part the most successful (and labour-saving) 'pot and pan' gardening I undertook was to plant the early-flowering, jewel-like Kabschia saxifrages in an old, cracked piece of industrial earthenware, before plastic replaced such homely and shapely objects. Within it, they prospered with little attention, year after year.'

Sundials

The ancients told the time by the slowly creeping shadows cast by the circling sun, and at night by the motion of the moon. Sundials are surely the oldest of all chronometers, and the shadows of their gnomens have told the time for centuries. They were the only time-keepers, until the coming of the inexorable tick-tock that now rules our lives: furthermore they have acted as useful decoration in gardens since gardens began.

Charles Lamb was fascinated by sundials, and wrote in *The Essays of Elia* about the 'antique air' of the almost effaced sundials of the Inner Temple 'with their moral inscriptions, seeming coevals with that Time which they measured', and he notes how, as a child he would watch 'the dark line steal imperceptibly on, eager to detect its movement, never catched, nice as an evanescent cloud, or the first arrests of sleep'. In comparison, he thought, 'what a dead thing is a clock, with its ponderous embowelments of lead and brass, its pert or solemn dullness of communication, compared with the simple altar-like structure and silent heart-language of the old sundial'.

For Lamb, a sundial 'spoke of moderate labours, of pleasures not protracted after sunset, of temperance, and good hours. It was the primitive clock, the horologe of the first world. The shepherd "carved it out quaintly in the sun"; and, turning philosopher by the very occupation, provided it with mottoes more touching than tombstones.'

There are many telling legends for sundials, aphorisms which point a moral, and express, with only some sanctimony, the sentiments evoked by passing time. One of the best mottoes of all—hopeful and to the point—must surely be '*Horas non numero nisi serenas*', 'I only tell of sunny hours'. Best known '*Tempus fugit*', or with a touch of gallic melancholy,

1 A sundial on a simple but suitably massive stone base in the walled rose-garden at Pusey House in Berkshire
2 'I only tell of sunny hours'. A wall sundial on a house in Essex
3 An armillary sphere, a skeleton celestial globe, makes effective garden decoration. Such spheres were once used in the study of the stars

1

'*Elle fuit, hélas*', jolliest, '*À la bonne heure*'. Most disagreeable 'Time wastes you, do not waste it', and, downright sinister, a motto that the editor of this book found inscribed on a sundial in a deserted garden in Scotland, 'It's later than you think'.

There are sundials which survive in Scottish gardens far older than any that are to be seen in the south—perhaps because Scotland was always a poorer country than England, and the Scottish did not follow so closely the changing fashions of the seventeenth and eighteenth centuries. At Drummond Castle there is a monumental ten-sided dial (page 188) which tells the time, not only in Perthshire, but in Paris, Rome and Constantinople.

Time has often been personified by an old man with a scythe or sickle, 'Father Time'. There is a sundial in this form at St. Paul's Waldenbury in Hertfordshire (page 185). In the eighteenth century less ornate sundials were the fashion. These were usually supported on simple balusters, such as several illustrated on these pages.

Sundials make the ideal centre point for a formal rose garden, or at

2

the junction of four paths. They should find a place in every garden—but, of course, it must be a place in the sun. They look best standing on firm bases, even if, in *Alice in Wonderland*, the sundial stood, not on stone but on a grass plot—a wabe ('wabe', according to Humpty Dumpty, 'because it goes a long way before it, and a long way behind it'). But that was in Wonderland, and in real life a sundial raised on a platform of some kind of stone or brickwork looks better and is more practical.

In a garden in Essex, well-known for many years to the editor of this book, there used to be a sundial surrounded by a circle of random paving planted with thyme, a pardonable horticultural pun.

Trompe L'oeil

The art, or artifice of *trompe l'oeil* should be used with the greatest circumspection in the garden, where, above all else, Nature and reality are to be respected.

The false perspective can certainly be telling when seen for the first

1 This path in trompe l'oeil 'planned to create an illusion of length, can only achieve its effect when approached from the broader end'
2 A London garden doubled in size by a panel of mirror glass, framed with bamboo plants

1 A panel of mirror glass, strategically placed behind a wrought iron gate, suggests another garden beyond
2 Two suspended stars shed their light on an ivy-clad tree. The sources of light used to floodlight a garden, if attractive in themselves, need not always be hidden

time—and even more important, when seen from the premeditated angle. But the path, such as the one shown on page 170, which is planned to create an illusion of length, can only achieve its effect when approached from the broader end. It may be that *trompe l'oeil*, to be successful in a garden, should either be flagrantly artificial, and therefore not really *trompant* at all, or totally deceiving like the ha-ha, which is always successful in its object of enlarging boundaries and co-opting the surrounding countryside. But even a sunk fence can elicit few ha-ha's of surprise when seen for the second time. And between the two extremes one hesitates. Mr. Martin Newell's stylish obelisk (page 191) in painted ply-wood is a charming conceit—a toy in fancy—but one cannot help thinking how much more impressive it would have looked in real stone. On the other hand his big wall-painting on the same page seems totally successful. One knows it could not possibly be real, but one can acclaim its decorative value. The exercise in *trompe l'oeil* in trellis work shown on page 130 would be arresting the first time one saw it, but perhaps afterwards would be unsettling. Is it real or not? Could one accept the invitation to pass under that elegant arch, bear right to Elysian fields beyond? One realizes one could not, and yet the empty promise stands. It would surely end by being irritating.

Then there is the vexed question of the pro's and con's of the use of looking-glass in a garden—apart from the obvious complication of wear and weather. In the small town garden, an archway backed with mirror-glass and framed in ivy or woodwork can be most effective; especially if the glass is angled so as not to give the show away by reflecting the observer. Looking-glass used in such a way can certainly give the effect of enlarging gardens, and so is useful for small spaces. But the use of looking-glass in country gardens—where no lengthening of the view is usually necessary—seems exaggerated.

Lighting the Garden
In recent years there has been an entirely new development in the ornamenting of gardens—that of lighting them after dark. For Louis XIV's fêtes at Marly or Le Grand Trianon, thousands of candles in glass containers lit the scene. Later these were followed by Bengal lights and in Victorian days by Japanese lanterns, strung from tree to tree, as we see them in Sargent's famous picture of the beautiful Wyndham sisters, now in the Metropolitan Museum in New York. But compared to the new possibilities of electric flood lighting, these early efforts were amateurish indeed. How Le Nôtre, the Merlin who conjured the avenues of Versailles, would have seized on the possibility of floodlighting his *allées*. Except for high days and holidays the gardens at Versailles ceased to exist every evening at dusk. Had the Sun King been able to install electricity, Le Nôtre's great parterre and fountains might have made the most wonderful nocturnal spectacle imaginable. But even the Sun King

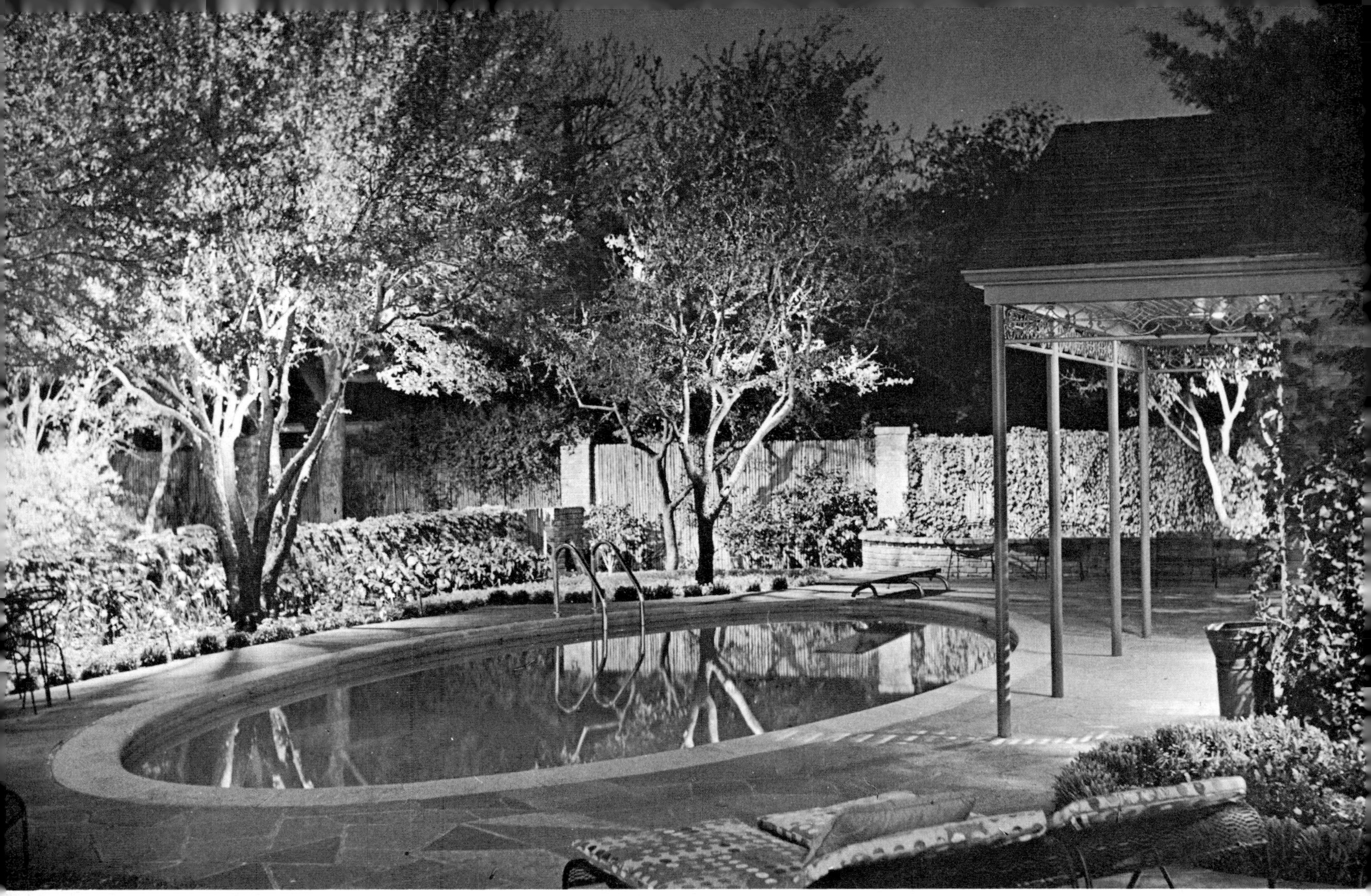

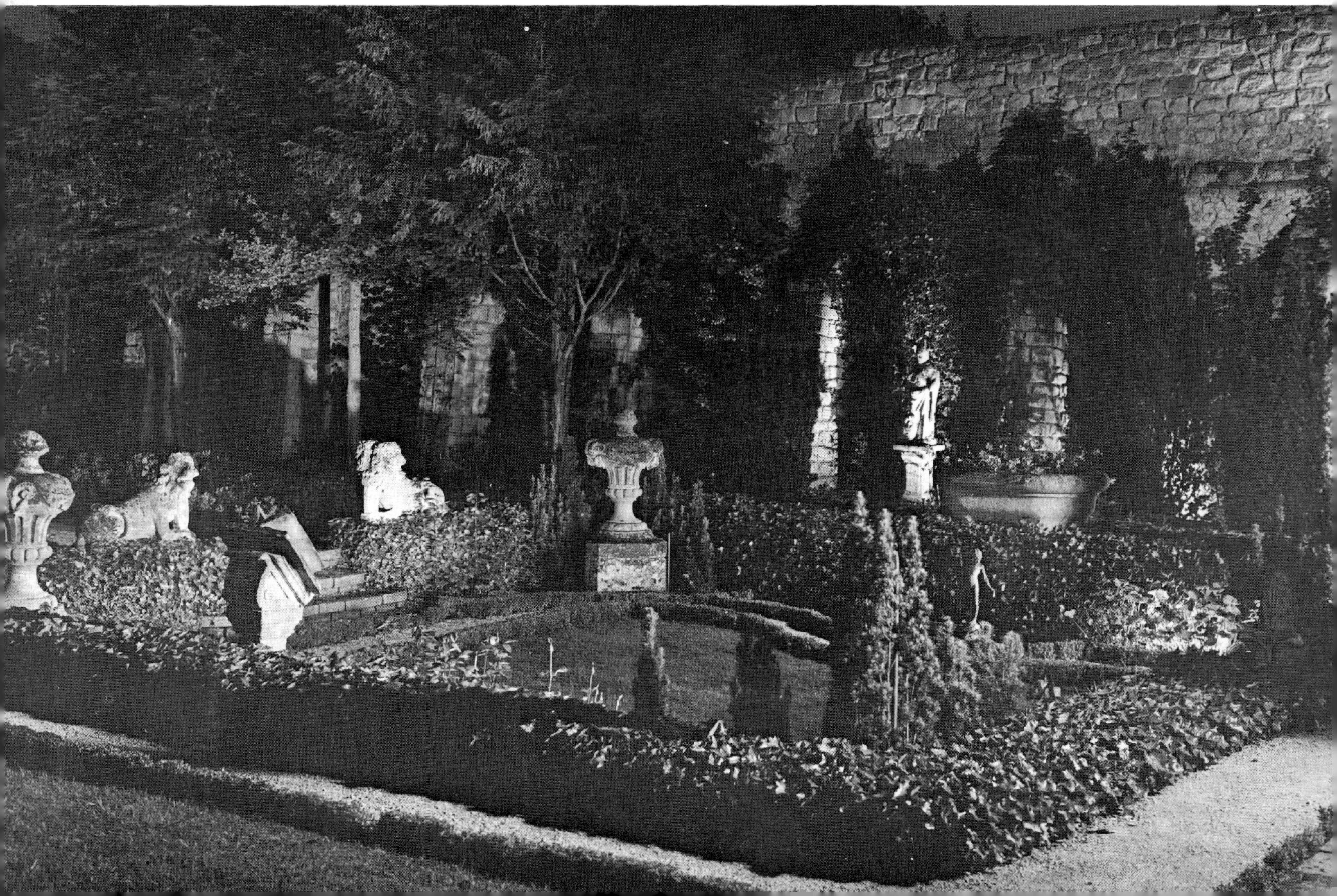

was unable to turn night into day, a power that modern invention has given to every housewife now, and at negligible cost. And one tree illuminated by one floodlight, can present a spectacle out of all proportion to the small increase to the electricity bill involved.

The most modest garden can become a place of magic if lit at night. A few sources of light only are required to enhance even the most ordinary of plots. Thus, a pencil-thin tree, such as a poplar, can be isolated against a black background by floodlighting; and a weeping willow looks incredibly beautiful with a light behind it. Most people's outdoor lighting is strictly functional and is to be found outside front doors, by garages, backyards and so on. But used decoratively, and with imagination, floodlighting can dramatize anything from a freshly-mown lawn, emerald green by artificial light, to the telling contrast of white tobacco flowers or lilies against a fretted background of green.

A spectacular effect can be achieved by a few, or even by one, carefully placed light. And there are several different approaches to the idea of lighting a garden at night. First of all, there is atmosphere lighting, which does not seek to show off any particular detail of the garden, but to give the whole scene an air of unity. Yellow light is good wherever there is greenery, while fluorescent white is more suitable for pathways and pools and pieces of water. The illumination of fountain jets makes the most of the power of light refraction on water.

Colour filters, if used with thought and tact, can heighten the effect of certain foliage; a blue filter, for instance, stresses the different tones of a blue cedar; an unfiltered light does the same with silver birches, and a red filter enhances copper beeches. But since these filters themselves absorb a great deal of the light, stronger bulbs must be used.

If several lights are used, the lamps should be of differing intensity and level; this greatly increases the effect. Care must be taken, too, that the heat of the bulbs does not wither any leaves in the immediate vicinity.

What special problems does outdoor lighting present? The main technical problem is to provide weatherproof equipment, which means sealed conduits for wiring, heavier cables, weatherproof fittings, sockets and, if necessary, outdoor switchgear. Aesthetically, the problem is to produce a fascinating effect while concealing the source of light.

Can the lighting be controlled from the house? The soundest arrangement is to run a sealed conduit under- or overground to a convenient point in the garden, tree base, shed or summerhouse, controlled from switches indoors, connected to the normal electricity supply. Cables can then be run off the weatherproofed socket fitting to small floodlight lamps placed at strategic points.

1 Overall floodlighting can make a garden a place of enchantment, especially in early summer when the foliage is still light green
2 Statuary takes on a new role when lit up at night. The presiding statue in this French garden is of Saint Fiacre, patron saint of gardeners
3 Single trees and shrubs can make a fairy-like effect when simply spot-lit

1

2

3

175

1   2   3

5

6

7

1 Startlingly realistic statuary by the lake at Château de St. Brice near Cognac in France. Realism such as this, unless very tactfully employed, can detract from a garden's calm

2 A pair of white stag fountains at Schwetzingen near Mannheim, sculpted by Peter von Verschaffelt in the mid eighteenth century

3 The entrance to a lavender-hedged garden at Wilton in Wiltshire is guarded by sphinxes.

4 The garden of King Henry's Hunting Lodge near Odiham in Hampshire is given style by clipped laurels and two rustic eighteenth-century figures

5 A stone seat and an antique lion's head give character to a corner of this garden at Silver End in Essex

6 A fine pair of stone dogs on the garden terrace at Basildon Park in Berkshire

7 Rousham, in Oxfordshire, has one of the few surviving gardens laid out by William Kent (1685–1748). It is embellished with many of its original eighteenth century statuary and pavilions. Here are shown a heroic sculpture and one of Kent's elegant 'green-seats', originally 'bowling-green seats'

8 A shepherdess in Coade stone at Charlecote in Warwickshire. Coade stone is an artificial cast stone invented and marketed about 1770 by Mrs Eleanor Coade. The secret of making it is now said to be lost

8

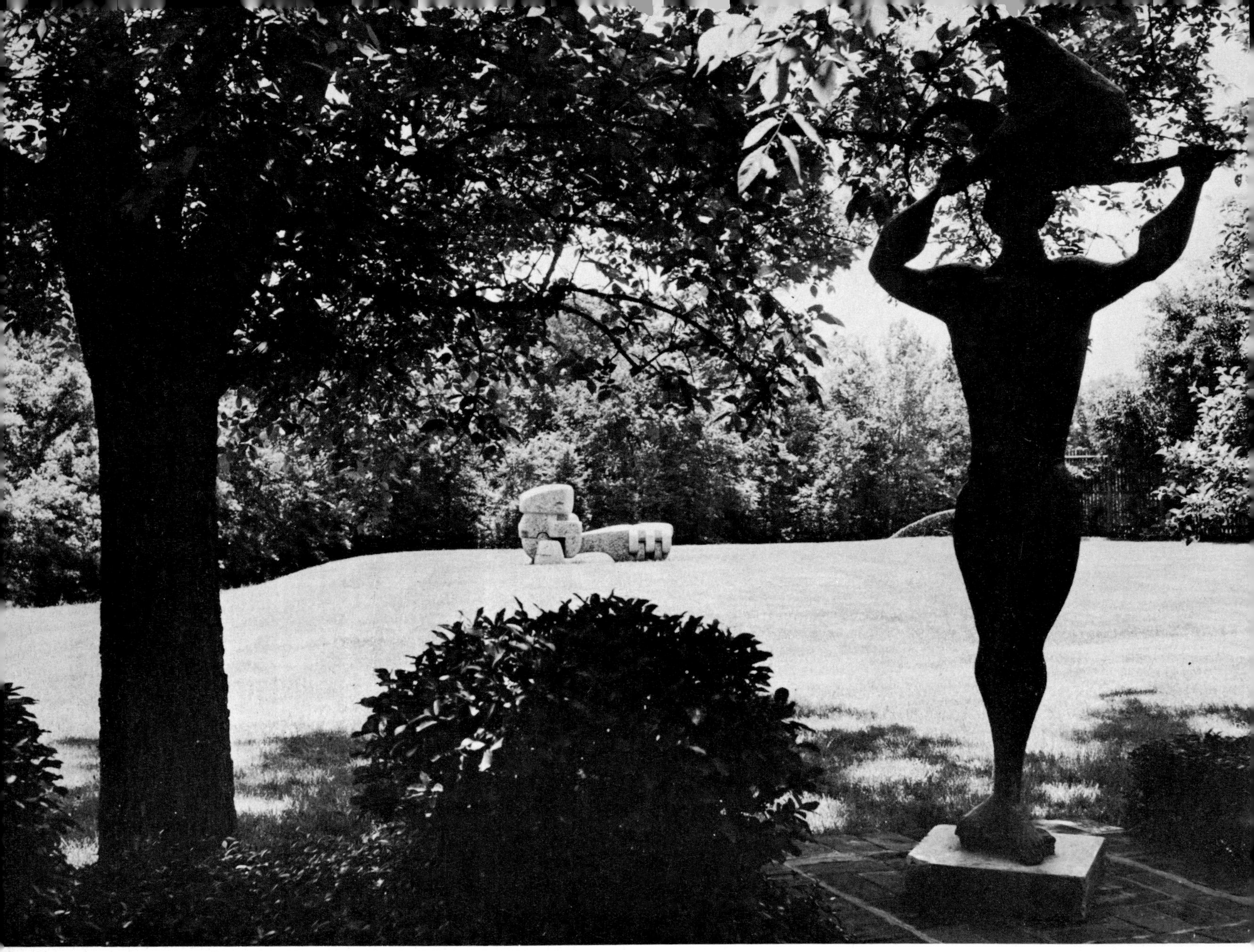

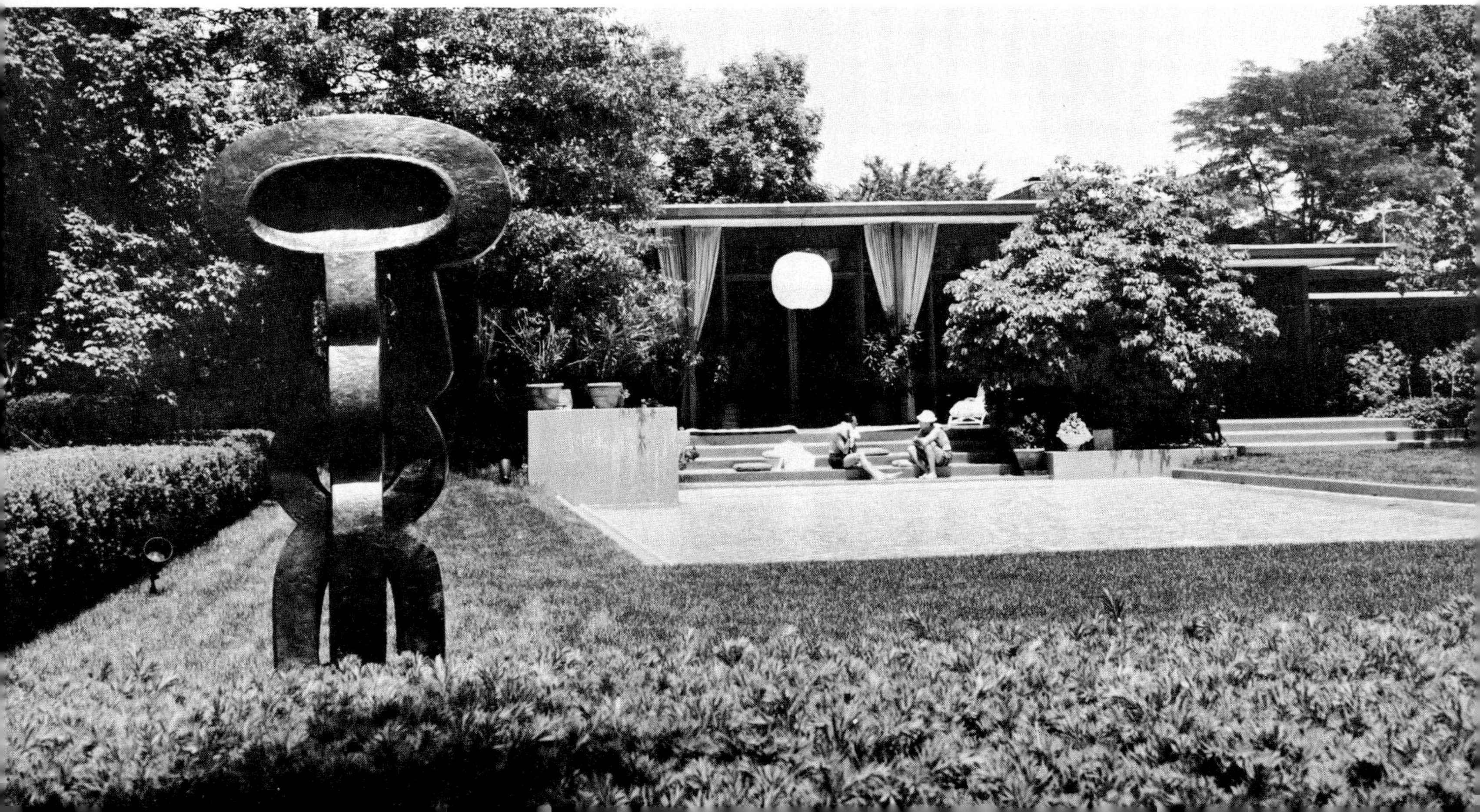

3

4

1 The bold outline of a sculpture by Luciano Minguzzi in a garden in St Louis, Missouri, is silhouetted against a background of fresh green lawn and leafy trees. Beyond is a rugged piece by Andrea Cascella

2 In a setting of grass, a clipped hedge and sheltering trees in the same garden, stands the totemic sculpture by Jacques Lipschitz—in silent contemplation of the nearby swimming pool

3 The slim watchful form of a sculpture by David Smith. It is named 'Sentinel'

4 Henry Moore's monumental hierarchic King and Queen throned on a windswept hillside of Mr. W. J. Keswick's Dumfriesshire estate

5 'Bronze Hammock' a striking sculpture by Michael Ayrton slung from a lime tree in a St. John's Wood garden

5

1 A recumbent figure in composite stone symbolizing the Atlantic, once in the garden of the Crystal Palace, is effectively sited over the infant River Hamble at Hatchmans near Henley

2 One of the gay statues of dressed-up children which frolic in the rococo garden at Veitshöchheim, near Würzburg. They are from the witty, light-hearted chisel of Ferdinand Dietz

3 Giant oil jars, neatly laid paving and a gracefully draped statue decorate the lime walk at Sissinghurst Castle in Kent

4 At Drummond Castle in Perthshire there is one of the grandest formal parterres in Scotland, with fine Italian statuary and well-tailored topiary

1 A symphonic combination of silver grey, green and white in a Paris garden. The sculpture is by Arp
2 Henry Moore's great bronze 'Reclining Woman' is raised on a paved platform amid trees in the Alan Wurtzburger garden at Stevenson, Maryland

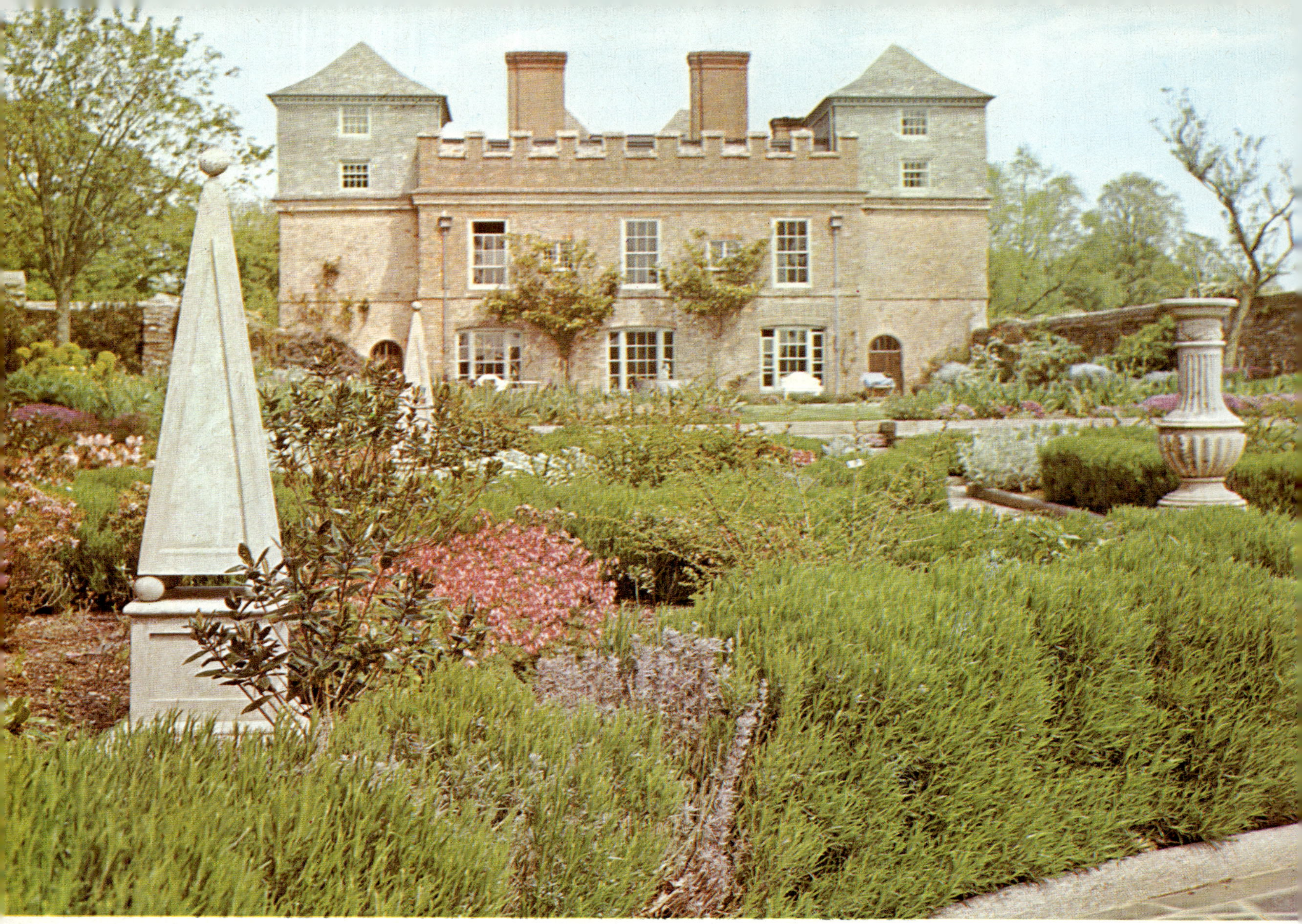

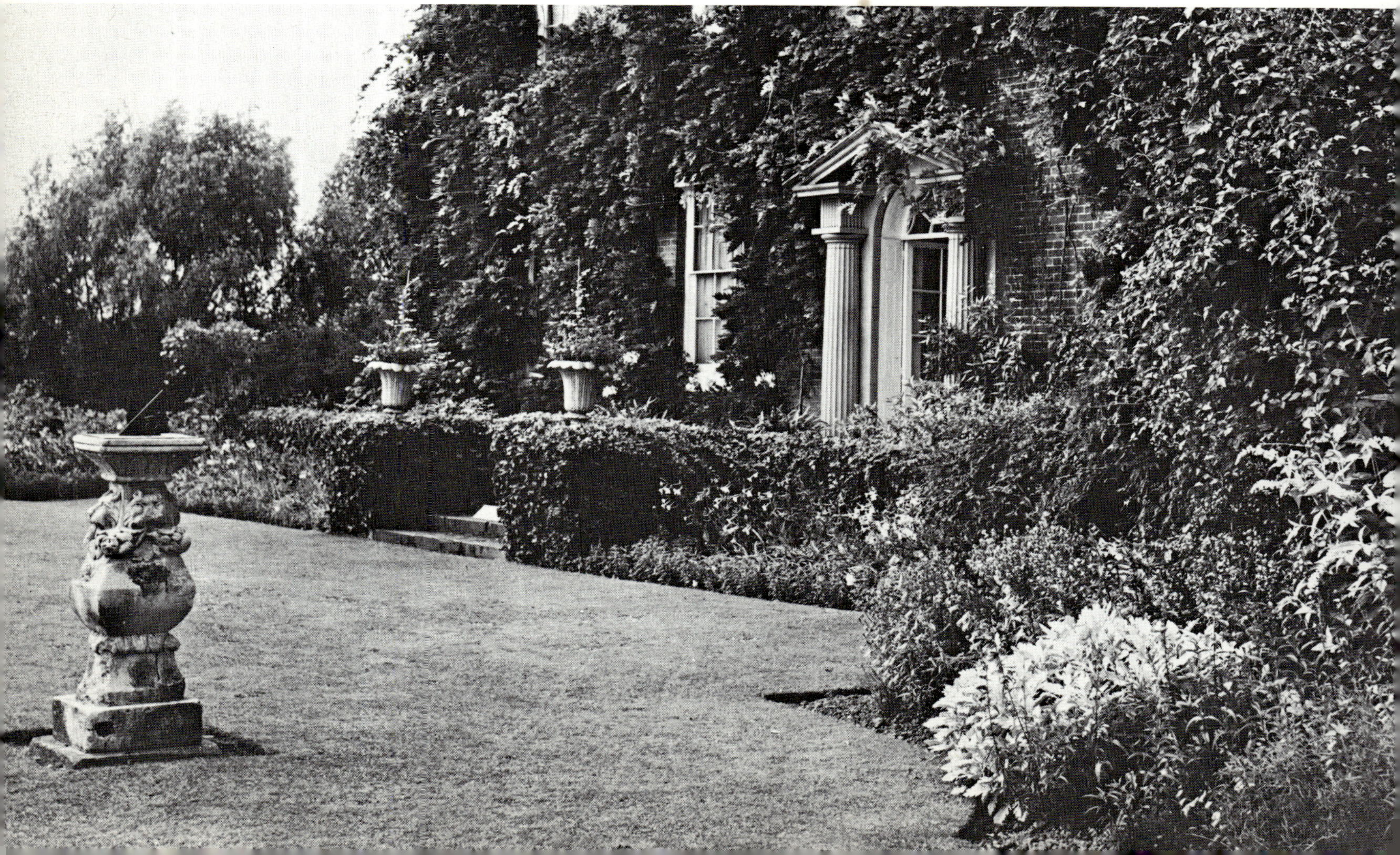

3

4

1 Obelisks and a sundial in the closely-planted garden at Ince Castle in Cornwall

2 A sundial on a swagged baluster in a well-planted Herefordshire garden; a wider base might give it more importance

3 A ship-surmounted orrery in a snowy scene at Puttenham Priory near Guildford

4 'Time has often been personified by an old man with a scythe or sickle . . . Father Time'. An eighteenth century sundial at St. Paul's Walden Bury in Hertfordshire

5 A sundial in terracotta with the luxuriant leaves of Bergenia crassifolia clothing its base. Sempervivums, said to ward off evil spells, grow round the dial

6 'And children bear the weight of times unknown'. A sundial in a setting of roses and old brick walls in Wiltshire

5

6

1 A small town garden can be given character and charm by the addition of a simple statue or a vase of flowers such as these

2 Strawberry jars planted either with strawberries or, as here, with mixed flowers look well stood out on a terrace

3 Terrace pots should be simple in outline so as not to detract from the beauty of the plants grown in them

4 Many Italian villas of the Renaissance period have grottos of tufa and inlaid panels of mosaic; usually they contain a fountain or dipping pool, and are picturesquely overgrown with ferns

5 'Some of the most beautiful I know are the basket work pots that stand on the garden stairway at Powis Castle'. These two are planted with geraniums and dracaenas

6 A stone vase decorated with swags of fruit, and planted with geraniums

7 Terrace pots should be generously planted, but the luxuriance and quality of the flowers depends on a rich soil mixture, good drainage, and regular watering

8 Recently, terrace pots have been made in fibre glass, a light, modern material which looks something like lead. Made from moulds of eighteenth century models, containers in fibre glass can look most effective

9 Three classic white marble urns in a setting of yew hedges make the angle of the terrace at the Villa Marlia near Lucca, once the country palace of Napoleon's sister, Elisa Bacciochi, while she was Grand Duchess of Tuscany. Elisa reopened the marble quarries at Carrara, of which the urns were probably a product

10 Swagged and crested vases of terracotta, planted to overflowing with pink geraniums and mauve Limonium profusum, by the swimming pool at Hever Castle in Kent, once the home of Anne Boleyn

1 'There are sundials which survive in Scottish gardens far older than any that are to be seen in the South'. At Drummond Castle in Perthshire

2 A flamboyant Japanese lantern in weathered copper and decorated with fish and dragons in the garden at Pylewell Park in Hampshire

3 Few objects of garden decoration are more fascinating than bonsai, or miniature trees, but it is important that the containers in which they grow should be in correct proportion

4 The Baroque pebble and water garden in the famous American garden at Dumbarton Oaks. It occupies the area that once was a tennis court, and the paving is kept damp to accentuate the colour of the stones

5 Carpet bedding to be successful should be kept simple, and not too many different plant materials used. This parterre is of close-clipped silver santolina and dark green box

1 The wall surrounding this elaborately pebble-paved courtyard has been painted to resemble a series of arches

2 A fountain on a floor of multi-coloured mosaic in one of the courtyard gardens of the Villa Taylor, in Marrakesh, where Roosevelt and Churchill held a momentous meeting in World War II

3 Trompe l'oeil in the garden must be carefully contrived if not to be irritating. This extravaganza, with its simulated fountain, is at Dumbarton Oaks

4 Decorative over-door panels—painted *en grisaille* by Hugh Robson—are striking features of the garden behind a mews house in Mayfair

5 A classical *frontone* in the Italian style with ball-capped finials, pillars of rusticated stone and a central 'statue'. Trompe l'oeil in the grand manner painted by Martin Newell to give importance to a London garden wall

6 Martin Newell also designed and painted this wooden obelisk in trompe l'oeil for the late Lady Juliet Duff, whose beautifully arranged garden at Bulbridge in Wiltshire was much admired

COLOUR AND FORM

Architectural plants, topiary and the bold use of colour, complete the furnishing of the well-designed garden

1 The sharp leaves of yucca contrasts with the pinnate foliage of Fatsia japonica against a screen of decorative concrete blocks at the Concrete Association's show garden at Wexham Springs near Slough

2 The soaring spires of Eremurus himalaicus are some of the most architectural of herbaceous flowers. Eremurus needs full sun, sharp drainage, space and protection from wind by a wall, as here, or a sheltering hedge

As pieces of sculpture or bronzes can embellish the well-furnished room there are certain plants which can, in the same way, embellish the well-furnished garden. These are plants of architectural form which give point and dignity to any corner of the garden in which they are planted. Many, though not all, are evergreens. So the evergreen—or evergrey—plants which might be described as architectural plants will be mentioned first.

The often-denigrated aucuba, in its dark-green form or A. crotonifolia, the golden variegated type, is not to be despised. No plant is more good-tempered, and all aucubas will grow in deep shade and poor soil. For town gardens they make a long-lasting background of green or gold—or both—against which, brighter but more fleeting, flowers can be displayed. Laurus nobilis, or bay—almost too well-known to stand in need of description—is surely the classic architectural plant. In tubs, and stood about in pots in a town garden, bays can give style to the simplest plot: moreover, their leaves are useful in cooking. Box (Buxus semperviren) still makes the most pleasing edging, and though, as mentioned elsewhere, it made Queen Anne sneeze, there is nothing so evocative and nostalgic on a hot afternoon as *l'odeur pénétrant des buis.* An attractive and original way to use box in a mixed border is not only as a straight edging but here and there in a simple scroll. The effect is completely artificial, and yet charming. All the eleagnus—the Wood Olives, which originate in China and Japan, are architectural plants of value; ebbingii has silvery foliage, and blends well with plantings of darker evergreens, such as laurel or yew—while pungens aurea variegata is one of the very best furnishing plants in the garden, with its large leaves splashed with vivid gold. For gardens on acid soil, a plant of fine form which will make an impressive sight in a natural setting is Erica arborea—the Mediterranean Tree Heath. It has dense dark foliage

2

This impressive topiary garden is at Haseley Court in Oxfordshire. In it giant chessmen of box, Irish Yew and standard laurel provide the green, while low plantings of santolina and Stachys lanata give contrasting silvers. During the war, when the rest of the garden had to be neglected, a devot-

ed gardener never failed to clip these chessmen which he referred to, with affection, as his 'kings and queens'. Cattle graze beyond the ha-ha

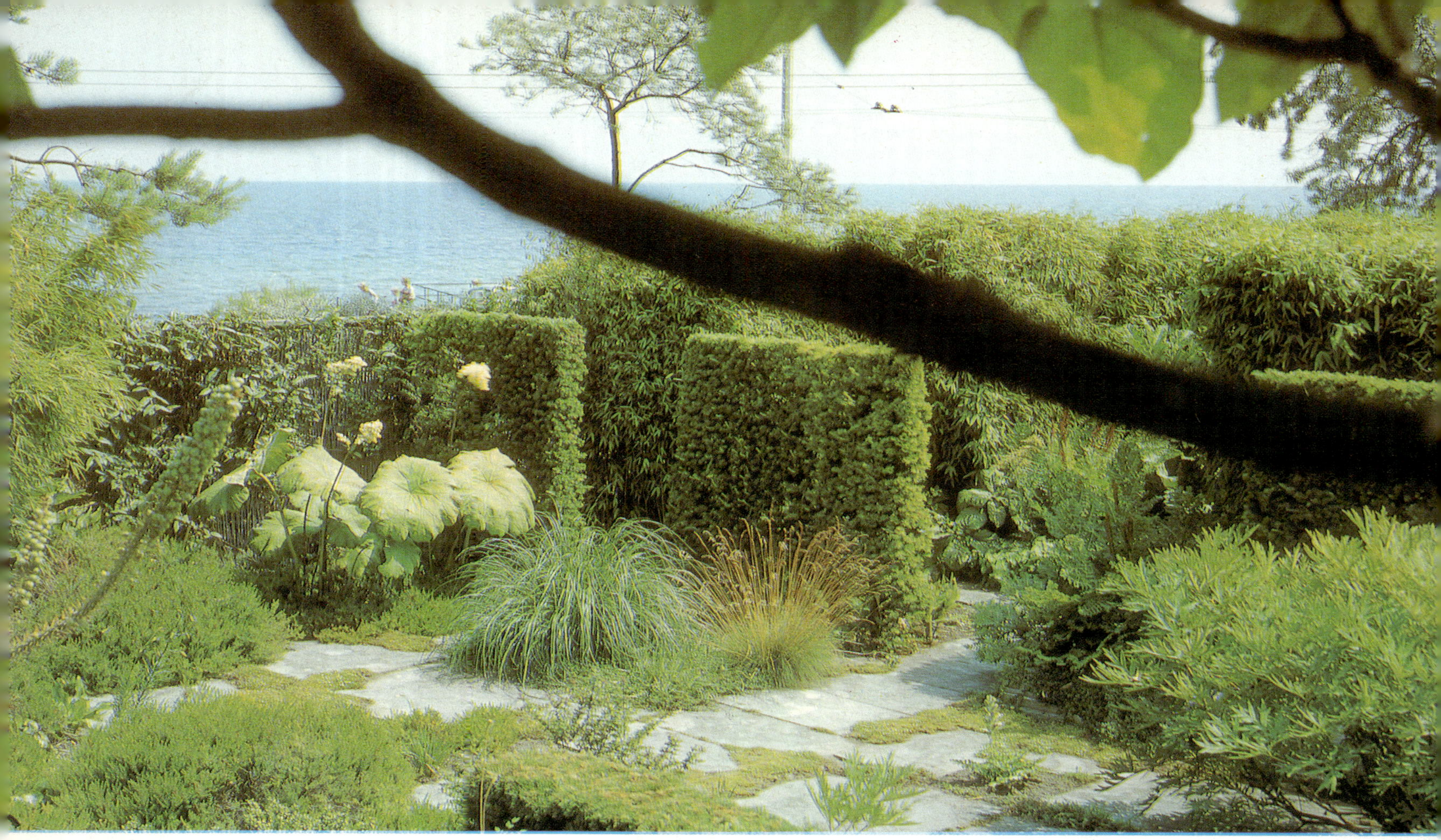

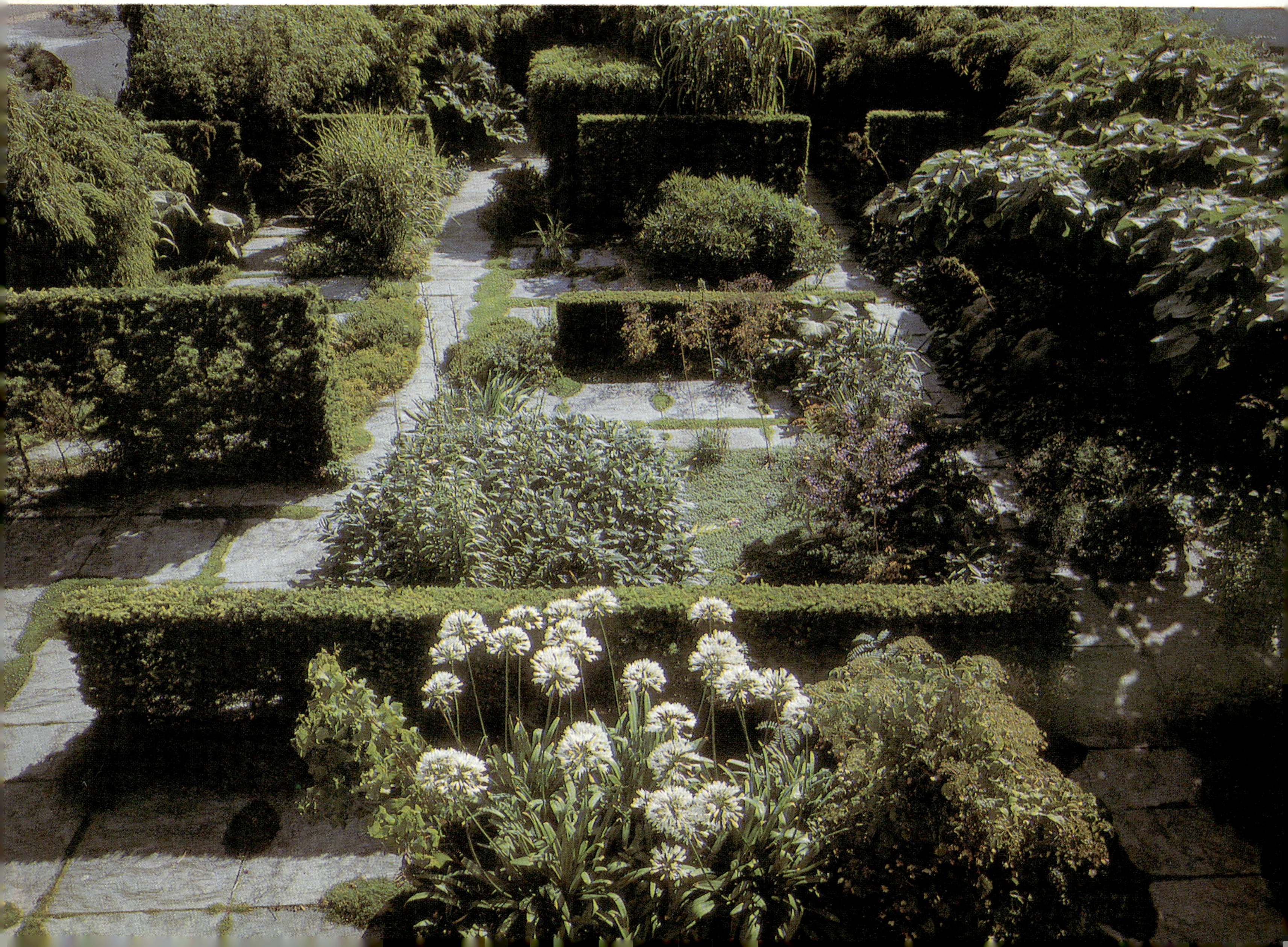

and rose-pink, honey-scented flowers. Euphorbia wulfenii, a giant shrubby spurge is a very good-looking furnishing plant, and it has acid green flowers which persist for months.

Many people are allergic to Fatsia japonica, page 192, perhaps because its good nature leads it to be planted in dismal positions where nothing else, not even laurels, can be expected to be happy—but fatsia is a fine fellow with its vast, palmate leaves of glossy dark green: and its white flowers in umbels, borne in autumn, have character, too. No list of architectural plants would be complete without Garrya elliptica. The pendant catkins of this shrub are often said to have inspired the Adam brothers with their swag designs—though this can hardly be so, as garrya was first known in England thirty years after the Adam brothers were dead. Only the male form of garrya sports the long silky catkins which are the plant's special beauty, and these are shown to perfection if the shrub is planted against a wall.

Veronicas or hebes can supply the soft furnishings, rather than the sculpture of the garden. Autumn Glory, cupressoides (with leaves like those of a Cypress), La Seduisante, not quite hardy but with beautiful purple leaves, and traversii, a good plant for town gardens, are all hebes which, all year round, provide a comfortable, well-furnished look.

Hollies are always favourite plants, and argentea marginata and Golden King are two of the best. In the depths of winter, both of these outstanding hollies can provide a garden with a certain sparkle. Lavender can supply the cushions of the well-furnished garden—and Lavandula vera, or Dutch lavender, is the one to choose, for not only has it got the usual fragrant lavender flowers, but it has softer, more silvery foliage than that of English lavender.

Ligustrum—like aucuba—is a shrub which thoughtless gardeners sniff at. Privet, they say with disdain—and turn away. But L. aureum, the Golden Privet, if rightly placed, is a magnificent plant—and for Miss Gertrude Jekyll it was 'one of the few shrubs that have a place in the flower border. The clear, cheerful, bright yellow gives a note of just the right colour all through the summer. It also has a solidity of aspect that enhances, by contrast . . .' the more feathery outline of neighbouring plants. For town gardens Golden Privet is a godsend and can brighten many a dark corner.

Olearia, osmanthus, pittosporum, pyracantha, and phlomis are five other shrubs which are fully evergreen, and can supply a solid mound of foliage to contrast with other plants around. Phlomis is one of the best, with grey, felted leaves, and pittosporum, if the climate is not too ___ can provide year-long green which always looks bright and ___

___ dendrons if planted not in the wild garden, but used archi-t___ly as points of interest for a formal parterre, can look wonderful___pulent; while rosemary (said never to grow higher than a man) is

1, 2 Two views of a garden in Denmark which is well furnished with hedges and well-chosen plant material rather than with statues or architecture. In it neat hedges of yew and plantations of bamboo shelter tree paeonies, agapanthus and large leaved rheums from the breezes off Copenhagen Sound. The owner of the garden is Architect Arne Jacobsen
3 'Verbascum giganteum, grown to its full height of seven foot, fairly illuminates the scene with its candelabra of bright gold flowers'
4 For a damp situation, and where its invasive growth can be controlled, there are few more impressive plants than the large form of petasites, P. japonicus, with its floating light green leaves following pale rose flowers

1 *Ars topiaria* was practised by the Romans, and is as popular a garden decoration now as it was in Pliny's day. These massive yews and sloping knot gardens in box are at Airlie Castle near Kirriemuir

2 In late summer the discerning gardener who has planted Yucca gloriosa (Adam's Needle) is rewarded by some of the most imposing flower spires in the garden

3 One of the most imposing of all architectural plants is Heracleum mantegazzianum, or Giant Hemlock; it can grow over ten feet high

one of the best of all evergreen shrubs to provide form and shape and furniture for a garden.

Ruta graveolens, Jackmans Blue, is a wonderful new plant with leaves which offer the most startling blue of any other foliage plant. It will stand through all but the hardest winters, and benefits from being cut down hard in March. Santolina, salvia and senecio are three other stalwart plants which make the framework of many of the best-planted gardens of today. They are three shrubs which year after year will give of their best, providing pillows of silver leaves which are the perfect and permanent foil for brighter but more transient flowers. The gold and purple forms of salvia are particularly beautiful plants. Skimmia is a good upholstery plant of neat form, with glossy leaves, and spectacular berries. It is necessary, for a good show of these, to plant both the male and the female form: and the same rule applies to another furnishing shrub Viburnum davidii, a beautiful Chinese plant which, if its private life is well arranged, produces bright blue berries every autumn.

A spectacular evergreen plant which can act as an exclamation mark in any border is the New Zealand Flax—Phormium tenax (page 204). There is a good purple form. Our last architectural, evergreen plant must, after Phormium tenax, be the most spectacular of all: Yucca gloriosa, or filamentosa. These natives of Mexico will grow quite happily in northern gardens: and if given good drainage can produce one of the most noble silhouettes in the border. A yucca in full flower, in late summer, is an impressive sight.

2

Herbaceous Plants of Architectural Shape

There are fewer herbaceous plants of truly architectural value than there are evergreen, but a few which the discerning gardener—looking for good leaf-form and a certain grandeur of outline—should remember when furnishing his garden are, first, acanthus, which is surely the architectural plant *par excellence*. It inspired the Greek architects in their invention of the Corinthian capital, and its handsome, deeply-indented leaves have figured in carvings and friezes for centuries. Its flower spikes too, with their strange, rather sinister colouring, are magnificent. The silver leaves of the artemisias give colour and form to the border, and act as a splendid foil for brighter colours. Lambrook Silver is the least invasive of this ground-hungry group. Bergenias are plants which were acclaimed for their architectural quality by Miss Gertrude Jekyll, who often used them, especially associated with paving, in her garden plans—Bocconias are truly herbaceous, and unlike bergenias die back completely in winter. But in July, with their pink and cream coloured sprays of flowers high aloft over their olive green, Ace-of-Clubs leaves, bocconias present an impressive picture. There is no plant better suited to fill a corner in the back row of the border, and they are especially effective against a background of evergreens.

The herbaceous euphorbias show mounds, or rather cushions, of bright yellow flowers in early spring, and hostas are very popular with garden planners today (see page 200 for both). Though almost too low-growing to be called architectural, they cover the ground as

3

1 Euphorbia wulfenii, a plant of impressive outline, shows a mass of acid-green flower heads in early spring. To the right, the indented foliage of Rheum palmatum

2 'Almost too low-growing to be called architectural . . .' Hosta fortunei marginato alba makes a fine explosion of leaves, and is an efficient weed suppressor

3 The gnarled boles of old nut trees make fine furniture for a garden. These, at Fingringhoe Hall in Essex are under-planted with a wall-to-wall carpet of large-flowered polyanthus

well as any other plant, and their glaucous leaves, greenish blue in colour, look fresh and cool for months on end. They like half shade and damp. Sedum telephium, Autumn Joy, is a new plant which has quickly won popularity—architectural? Well, it looks good from June on through until October when its great russet heads are at their best—and it is a capital weed suppressor. Lastly, the verbascums. All this family, whether the biennial varieties such as giganteum and the white flannelled bombyciferum, or the truly perennial Pink Domino and Cotswold Queen, are magnificent tall plants, with the curious talent that some plants have, not only of furnishing a border, but in some way giving it distinction. Verbascum giganteum, grown to its full height of seven feet, fairly illuminates the scene with its candelabra of bright gold flowers, as can be seen on page 197.

Topiary

For gardeners who cannot have too many growing things in their gardens—who resent the space taken by statuary in lead or stone—topiary provides the contrast in form at which every thoughtful garden-planner aims.

Topiary work—*Ars topiaria*—was first used in English gardens in the time of Henry VIII, though it was known and practised a thousand or so years before; and in Roman gardens there were bushes of box clipped into the shapes of birds, animals and initials.

Though topiary work can be exaggerated and unfortunate—yew trees are obviously not ideally suited to be cut into such shapes as motorcars or teapots—traditional topiary can prove impressively sympathetic against a background of old trees. The great topiary garden at Haseley Court (pages 194 and 195) offers a prime example.

Topiary and well-clipped hedges are well-suited to the embellishment of large gardens and cottage gardens alike. They provide the perfect background for the colours of flowers and the leaf form of plants. This evergreen architecture, though it does not share, in the words of Sir George Sitwell, in 'the hopes of spring and the regrets of autumn', offers a setting of tranquillity and maturity which is difficult to evoke, even in these days of press-button gardening.

A peacock in box or a Ganymede in lead? A pyramid of yew or a Venus in weathered stone? They are all sculpture in their way and, according to taste and choice, are worthy decorations for the well-furnished garden.

The Use of Colour

In recent years the thoughtful gardener, with room for such fancies, has planned borders in one colour. More than fifty years ago Gertrude Jekyll advocated this form of gardening. In her classic *Colour Schemes for the Flower Garden* she wrote enthusiastically about gardens of special colourings: 'It is extremely interesting to work out gardens in which

3

1, 2 That great gardener Gertrude Jekyll loved to plant gardens in one colour. She would certainly have approved this French garden in the heart of Paris planted with luminous white tulips, rhododendrons and Iberis sempervirens. In the distance, the dome of the Invalides

some special colouring predominates, and to those who, by natural endowment or careful eye-cultivation, possess or have acquired what artists understand by an eye for colour, it opens out a whole new range of garden delights.

'Arrangements of this kind are sometimes attempted, for occasionally I hear of a garden for blue plants, or a white garden, but I think such ideas are but rarely worked out with the best aims. I have in mind a whole series of gardens of restricted colouring, though I have not, alas, either room or means enough to work them out for myself, and have to be satisfied with an all-too-short length of double border for a grey scheme. But besides my small grey garden I badly want others, and especially a gold garden, a blue garden and a green garden; though the number of these desires might easily be multiplied.'

But Miss Jekyll goes on to point out that the idea must not be carried too far—or with too much rigidity. A blue border, just because of its name, can be immensely enhanced by the addition of some groups of white flowers. A red garden could tire the eye if its scarlets and crimsons had no silvers or bronzes to set them off.

Evergreens or evergreys are most useful plants for year-long colour and interest in the garden, and recently a follower in Miss Jekyll's formidable gardening boots (once the subject of a picture by the artist Sir William Nicholson)—Mary Lees—wrote, for *House & Garden*, a most interesting description of a border almost entirely of evergreens that she had recently planted. The site of the border had a background of trees, and her instructions were that the new planting was to be 'completely labour-saving and very largely evergreen'.

'In a design of this kind,' writes Mary Lees, 'the first—and obvious—necessity is "outline". The second is blending of colours, and, third, unevenness of planting heights.

'The highlight of the border is the clump of spear-like leaves of the variegated Phormium tenax which stands out well in the photograph (page 204). This holds the composition together, and has some golden privet planted behind it to throw it forward. For contrast, shrubs with dark green shining leaves are planted next to it.

'In front of the Senecio greyii, but not seen in the photograph, is a planting of dark red Acer japonica, one of the few deciduous plants in the border, and a clump of the variegated Iris foetidissima, a most useful plant for a border of this sort.

'In the foreground, beside the grey leaves of Senecio greyii, is the splendid gold foliage of the prostrate Euonymus radicans. Nearby, the bold outline of the Pittosporum tenuifolium stands out well, making a good background for a golden holly.

'I find the hebe family of the greatest value in this kind of work—H. lycopodioides is a marvellous sight throughout the year in my own garden in Devon. It looks like a brilliant golden cupressus, and I have planted it next to a grey-leaved cousin, H. traversii, which also keeps its foliage all the year round. Rhamnus alaternus variegata makes a good foil for these, particularly if planted with Cassinia fulvida, the lacy gold of the cassinia contrasting well with the leaves of the rhamnus.

'For those who object to "variegated" leaves, there are endless forms of green variegation in shape of leaves, and the variegated phormium has two useful relatives. The usual form has pale greenish-blue leaves, but best of all (although, unfortunately, tender) is the beautiful pinkish-bronze-leaved form, Phormium tenax atropurpureum. In my garden in Devon this is backed by a splendid cryptomeria—a picture in itself—with some scarlet large-leaved bergenia at its feet.

'On one side of the border is a fine specimen of Berberis bealei, and on the other side Rhododendron "Unique" with pink flowers maturing

1 A border, predominantly planted by Mary Lees in different coloured evergreens, evergolds and evergreys, to provide year-long interest. Among the differently textured foliage are those of golden cornus and eleagnus, grey senecio and purple Rhus cotinus.
2 Wood set in gravel makes an unusual groundwork in the Palm Garden at Elche, near Alicante in Spain. The plant is a giant agave with variegated leaves
3 Contrasting leaf-forms—iris and Hosta glauca in a close-set, and thus weed-free, border

1

to orange, and fresh green leaves. The whole border thus holds its colour and outline throughout the year, and I am assured that weeds are almost completely eliminated.'

Thus, Mary Lees, and one can see from the picture on page 204, how successful her border of evergreens was. It is a remarkable achievement and should teach gardeners to appreciate more the value of leaves, as well as flowers, for garden colour. Some of the plants shown on those two pages are not evergreen, but all can provide a garden with bright colour or striking form for at least three-quarters of the year.

In the well-planned garden at Hinton Ampner near Alresford in Hampshire, the owner has created a series of interlocking gardens which are full of interest all the year round. In the corner shown on page 91 neat steps of brick are clothed and curtained on either side with contrasting shrubs—most of which are evergreen. A severely clipped hedge of holly sets off the lapping sprays of Cotoneaster horizontalis. Behind grows Choisya ternata, a shiny-leaved evergreen, with pungent foliage. Though choisya originates in Mexico it will thrive in most English gardens, and, when it does, it rewards its grower with a mass of white flowers in spring. On the near balustrade of the steps is a deciduous vine, Vitis coignetiae, which colours well in autumn. The purple-leaved form is one of the best climbers one can grow. Its spring leaves are a fresh grey-green, deepening through the season to wine-red.

There is no better plant for cool silver colouring than the old-fashioned, ever-popular Stachys lanata, the Lambs Lug of cottage gardens. From early spring until late autumn it provides a weed-suppressing carpet of grey velvet leaves, and in summer it throws up a forest of woolly spikes of purple flowers. These are ideal for flower arrangements, in which they last for weeks on end. And as soon as the flowers are cut, the stachys spreads: one small plant in a season can cover an area a yard across—invaluable for 'young' gardens.

A small evergrey which is not often grown, and has silver foliage and pale yellow umbels of flower in June, is Helichrysum angustifolium. An attractive feature of this plant is the strong curry scent given off by its leaves if brushed against. Scrophularia nodosa variegata is another spectacular foliage plant which never entirely loses its leaves in winter. It gets its unalluring name from a belief, in the Middle Ages, that a poultice of its roots cured scrofula. Scrophularia likes light, not-too-dry soil and full sun. Its leaves are splashed with fresh green, cream and gold.

Asarum europaeum, asarabacca, or Wild Ginger is a ground-covering plant which seems only to be known to discriminating gardeners, and although this first-class plant has naturalized itself in some parts of England, it is grown in few gardens. It makes a tight mass of glossy kidney-shaped foliage—to the confusion of weeds and the great satisfaction of the gardener who has come to realize that a good leaf can give as much pleasure to the eye as a flower—and for far longer.

1 Santolina chamaecyparissus makes close silvery cushions of foliage. Behind are the imposing russet leaves and white flower spikes of Rheum palmatum atropurpureum
2 'The silent hours steal on' is the motto carved on this sundial, well-placed at the end of an avenue of Irish yews at Hinton Ampner in Hampshire

1

2

Printed and bound in England by Hazell, Watson & Viney Ltd, Aylesbury, Bucks